Time Out

LONDON
TOP 100

www.timeout.com

Time Out Guides Ltd
Universal House
251 Tottenham Court Road
London W1T 7AB
United Kingdom
Tel: +44 (0)20 7813 3000
Fax: +44 (0)20 7813 6001
Email: guides@timeout.com
www.timeout.com

Published by Time Out Guides Ltd, a wholly owned subsidiary of Time Out Group Ltd.
Time Out and the Time Out logo are trademarks of Time Out Group Ltd.
© **Time Out Group Ltd 2011**

10 9 8 7 6 5 4 3 2 1

London 2012 emblem(s) © The London Organising Committee of the Olympic Games
and Paralympic Games Ltd (LOCOG) 2007. All rights reserved.

This edition first published in Great Britain in 2011 by Ebury Publishing.
A Random House Group Company
20 Vauxhall Bridge Road, London SW1V 2SA

Random House Australia Pty Ltd 20 Alfred Street, Milsons Point, Sydney, New South Wales
2061, Australia

Random House New Zealand Ltd 18 Poland Road, Glenfield, Auckland 10, New Zealand

Random House South Africa (Pty) Ltd Isle of Houghton, Corner Boundary Road & Carse
O'Gowrie, Houghton 2198, South Africa

Random House UK Limited Reg. No. 954009

Distributed in the US and Latin America by Publishers Group West (1-510-809-3700)
Distributed in Canada by Publishers Group Canada (1-800-747-8147)

For further distribution details, see www.timeout.com.

ISBN: 978-1-84670-217-4

A CIP catalogue record for this book is available from the British Library.

Printed and bound by Firmengruppe APPL, aprinta druck, Wemding, Germany.

The Random House Group Limited supports The Forest Stewardship Council (FSC), the leading
international forest certification organisation. All our titles that are printed on Greenpeace
approved FSC certified paper carry the FSC logo. Our paper procurement policy can be found
at http://www.rbooks.co.uk/environment.

Time Out carbon-offsets its flights with Trees for Cities (www.treesforcities.org).

Contributors
The Editor would like to thank all contributors to the *Time Out London* guide and *1000 Things to do in London*, whose work forms the basis for parts of this book.

Maps john@jsgraphics.co.uk.

Cover Photography by Corbis.
Photography by pages 3, 30, 110 (right) Getty Images; pages 6, 107 Elisabeth Blanchet; pages 6 (top left), 7 (bottom right), 9, 18 (top left), 24, 27, 36/37, 39, 113 Britta Jaschinski; pages 6 (top right), 48, 49 (top right & bottom), 50/51, 140, 82/83 www.simonleigh.com; pages 6 (middle right), 136/137 Sarah Williams; pages 6 (bottom left), 9 (bottom right), 28, 29 (top right), 34, 38, 41, 44, 92/93, 103, 118 (left), 127, 144, 145 Michelle Grant; pages 7, 15, 17 (bottom left), 24 (right), 29, 58 (left), 74, 79, 80, 91 (top left), 100/101, 106, 116, 126 (top), 132, 141 (top) Jonathan Perugia; pages 7 (top left), 147 (bottom) Rama Knight/Wellcome Images; page 7 (bottom left) Jael Marschner; pages 9 (top left), 16, 52, 77, 84, 88, 90 Ben Rowe; pages 9 (middle left), 17 (bottom right), 22/23, 39 (top), 45, 47 (middle left), 110, 111, 122 Heloise Bergman; pages 11, 47 (top left), 54, 78 (left), 107 (top left) Ed Marshall; pages 12/13, 86/87 Giles Barnard; pages 17 (top left), 21, 102 (bottom right) Christina Theisen; page 17 (top right) David Axelbank; pages 18, 19, 40, 53, 56, 63, 67, 68 (left), 69, 74 (bottom left), 91 (top right), 102 (left), 135, 146 Rob Greig; page 21 (left) ODA 2008; pages 25, 81, 118 (right) Abigail Lelliott; pages 26, 30/32, 54/55 Olivia Rutherford; pages 31, 62, 130 Tove K Breitstein; pages 31 (top right), 39 (middle) Alys Tomlinson; pages 41 (bottom left), 57, 97 (top right), 130 (left) Michael Franke; pages 42/43, 147 (left) Oliver Knight; pages 45 (left & bottom), 141 (top), 152 (top left) Nick Ballon; pages 47, 96, 97 (bottom left), 107 (bottom left), 133 Ming Tang-Evans; pages 47 (bottom left), 85, 94/95, 102 (top right), 117 Andrew Brackenbury; page 49 Scott Wishart; page 58 (right) Sir John Soane's Museum; page 65 Alamy; page 67 (top left) Historic Royal Palaces/Newsteam; page 68 Marzena Zoladz; page 69 (right) Nigel Tradewell; page 70 Anthony Webb; page 72/73 copyright by kind permission of the Trustees of the Wallace Collection; page 76 Laurence Davis; page 78 (right) Katy Peters; page 85 (top left) Susannah Stone; page 91 Gordon Rainsford; page 97 Jitka Hynkova; pages 98,104/105, 121, 143 Photolibrary.com; page 99 John Tramper; page 110 (middle left) Wire Image; page 122 (bottom right) Alastair Muir; page 123 Christopher Duggan; pages 124/125 Leon Chew; page 126 (bottom) BBC/The Roundhouse; page 134 Royal Academy of Arts; page 138 (left) Derry Moore; page 138 Robert Harding Images/Masterfile; page 139 Emma Wood; page 142 Johan Persson; page 147 (top right) Julie Cockburn 2005/Wellcome Images; pages 148/149 Piers Allardyce; pages 150/151 Belinda Lawley; page 152 Scott Wishart.

The following images were provided by the featured establishments/artists: pages 20, 35, 59 (bottom right), 60/61, 89, 114/115, 131, 153.

© Copyright Time Out Group Ltd
All rights reserved

Introduction

As the UK capital gears up to host the London 2012 Olympic Games and Paralympic Games, there has never been a better time to visit. Now, more than ever before, visitors are spoilt for choice when it comes to deciding what to see and do.

To help you choose, *London Top 100* is Time Out's pick of the city's finest attractions, taking in museums, markets, galleries, shops, sporting attractions, city farms, parks, pubs, restaurants, bars and clubs – not to mention a whole host of London icons, from the scarlet-clad guards of Buckingham Palace to the much-loved British Museum. Whether you're into the chic shops of Marylebone or the stalls of Spitalfields Market, afternoon tea at the Wolseley or a slice of London's nightlife, we've got it covered.

GETTING AROUND
The back of the book contains street maps of central London, starting on p154. The majority of our top 100 sights and attractions are marked on the maps, with a key on p157.

THE LISTINGS
While every effort has been made to ensure the accuracy of the information contained in this guide, the publishers cannot accept responsibility for any errors it may contain. Businesses can change their arrangements at any time, and it is always advisable to phone ahead to find out opening hours, prices and other particulars.

TELEPHONE NUMBERS
All telephone numbers listed in this guide assume that you are calling from within London. If you're ringing from outside the city, you will need to use the area code (020) before the phone number. If you're calling from abroad, dial your international access code or a '+', then 44 for the UK; follow that with 20 for London, then the eight-digit number.

WHAT DO YOU THINK?
We welcome feedback on all of our guides, so please email any comments or suggestions to guides@timeout.com.

Time Out Guides is proud to be the official book publisher of travel and tourism guides for the **London 2012 Olympic Games and Paralympic Games**.

Best for...

A BIRD'S-EYE VIEW OF LONDON
Monument; no.23
St Paul's Cathedral; no.45
London Eye; no.49
Tower Bridge; no.50 ▶
Westminster Cathedral; no.60

LAZY SUNDAYS
BFI Southbank; no.18
Hampstead Heath; no.22
Spitalfields & Brick Lane; no.47
Royal Botanic Gardens
  (Kew Gardens); no.57
Eat at a gastropub; no.85
◀ Columbia Road Market; no.97

SPORTS FANS
Olympic Park; no.7
Wimbledon; no.13
North Greenwich Arena; no.42
Wembley Stadium; no.65
Lord's Cricket Ground; no.88 ▶

ENTERTAINING THE KIDS
London Dungeon; no.17
See fireworks; no.39
◀ Science Museum; no.46
HMS Belfast; no.52
Hyde Park & Kensington Gardens;
  no.53
Natural History Museum; no.83

FINDING A BARGAIN
Topshop; no.29
Camden Market; no.37
Spitalfields & Brick Lane; no.47
Eat well for less; no.59
Portobello Market; no.67 ▶

QUIRKY COLLECTIONS
Horniman Museum; no.14
Sir John Soane's Museum;
    no.32
Old Operating Theatre, Museum
    & Herb Garret; no.35
Hunterian Museum; no.74
◄ Wellcome Collection; no.96

ICONIC LONDON EXPERIENCES
Walk the Thames Path; no.26
Saunter through Soho; no.56
Ride the Routemaster; no.62
Horse Guards Parade & the
    Changing of the Guard; no.77
Trafalgar Square; no.82 ►
Buckingham Palace & the Royal
    Mews; no.89

RAINY AFTERNOONS
Victoria & Albert Museum;
    no.3
◄ British Museum; no.9
Museum of London; no.33
Wallace Collection; no.43
Westfield London; no.55
Wellcome Collection; no.96

A TASTE OF LONDON LIFE
Borough Market; no.5 ►
Chinatown; no.25
Sample the best of British;
    no.31
Fortnum & Mason; no.41
Eat at a gastropub; no.85

A MOMENT OF CALM
Chelsea Physic Garden; no.11
Dulwich Picture Gallery; no.34
Wallace Collection; no.43
Have a pint; no.44
◄ Highgate Cemetery; no.87

The ultimate guide to London – it's official

SERIOUS SHOPPING

Hit the shops in Marylebone; no.19
Topshop; no.29
Westfield London; no.55
Splash out at London's
  department stores; no.71 ▶

WILDLIFE-WATCHERS

St James's Park; no.1
◀ ZSL London Zoo; no.4
WWT London Wetland Centre;
  no.48
Sea Life London Aquarium;
  no.95

URBAN SOPHISTICATES

Take afternoon tea; no.20
Fortnum & Mason; no.41
Splash out at London's
  department stores; no.71
Sip a cocktail; no.94 ▶

ART APPRECIATION

◀ National Portrait Gallery; no.8
Whitechapel Gallery; no.21
Somerset House; no.27
National Gallery; no.58
The Tates; no.75
Royal Academy of Arts; no.86
Saatchi Gallery; no.90

A TOP NIGHT OUT

Comedy Store; no.6
Go clubbing; no.12 ▶
All Star Lanes; no.24
Sample the Camden scene;
  no.81
See a West End show; no.92
Sip a cocktail; no.94

The best
of London

London
Top 100

1 St James's Park

The most central Royal Park is also one of London's most charming green spaces. **St James's Park** (7298 2000, www.royalparks.org.uk) may be small, but the waterfowl lake that runs through its centre is a source of endless delight, with its splay-footed, barking coots and five mischievous pelicans. A few years ago, one of the pelicans was caught on camera as it swallowed a passing pigeon; in general, though, the birds stick to a diet of fresh fish. If you want to see them gulping their lunch down, feeding time is at around 2.30pm daily.

Buckingham Palace overlooks the western edge of the park, and Horse Guards Parade opens up to the east – no wonder the London 2012 Marathon route will be circling the park. Between them, **Inn The Park** (7451 9999, www.innthepark.com) is a polished all-day eaterie; breakfast on buttermilk pancakes on the lovely terrace, pop into the self-service café for lunch, or dine on seasonal British dishes in the restaurant.

2 | Tower of London

The Tower's craggy walls guard all sorts of grisly delights, from displays detailing the gruesome end of traitors to the Royal Armoury's swords, poleaxes, morning stars (spiky maces) and cannons. The Yeoman Warders – popularly known as Beefeaters – have lurid tales to tell on their free, hour-long tours too. Less bloodthirsty visitors can admire the glittering Crown Jewels (get there early to avoid long queues) and the beautiful Medieval Palace, with its reconstructed bedroom, throne room and tranquil private chapel.

Tower Hill, EC3N 4AB (0844 482 7777, www.hrp.org.uk).
Tower Hill tube or Tower Gateway DLR.

ENTRY TO THE TRAITORS GATE

3 Victoria & Albert Museum

Behind the V&A's imposing exterior lie seven floors of treasures, which span the worlds of art, design, photography, theatre and textiles. From benign-faced Buddhas to a life-size automated tiger, architectural drawings to monumental plaster casts of towering ancient columns, the collections are as varied as they are magnificent.

Highlights include seven Raphael Cartoons, painted in 1515 as tapestry designs for the Sistine Chapel, and the 16th-century Ardabil carpet, the world's oldest and possibly most splendid floor covering. Don't miss the stunning collection of Italian Renaissance sculpture in the reworked Medieval & Renaissance Galleries, which includes Giambologna's masterful, twisting *Samson Slaying a Philistine* and an entire gallery devoted to Donatello's works.

For advice on how best to negotiate the museum's riches, consult the ever-patient staff, who field a formidable combination of leaflets, gallery floorplans, general knowledge and polite concern – and if it all becomes too much, stop for a breather in the magnificent Victorian refreshment rooms.

Cromwell Road, SW7 2RL (7942 2000, www.vam.ac.uk). South Kensington tube.

▶ *For a fresh perspective on the collections – and a glass of wine – head to one of the V&A's brilliant Friday Late events; see no.72.*

Inquisitive monkeys, gorgeously patterned pythons and spindly stick insects – London Zoo has something for everyone. Gorilla Kingdom, the lions of Big Cats and, right by the entrance, the Penguin Pool are all on the must-do list, but the meerkats, lemurs and giant anteaters are hard to resist too. A packed programme of live animal events keeps the kids entertained, whether it be a hands-on encounter with a bird-eating spider in BUGS, or an opportunity to admire prodigiously digging aardvarks in Animal Adventure, the new children's zoo.

Regent's Park, NW1 4RY (7722 3333, www.zsl.org). Baker Street tube, or Camden tube then bus 274, C2.

Temptation is all around at this sprawling food market: head out hungry to take advantage of abundant free samples of rare-breed charcuterie and fine cheeses, fragrant olive oils, cakes and pies. Highlights might include Spanish specialist Brindisa's chorizo and rocket rolls, Flour Power City Bakery's dense chocolate brownies and Kappacasein's amazing toasted cheese sarnies – Montgomery cheddar, onions, leeks, garlic and Poilâne sourdough bread. The hordes descend on Saturdays; to avoid the crush, visit on Thursday or Friday afternoon.
Southwark Street, SE1 (7407 1002, www.boroughmarket.org.uk). London Bridge tube/rail.

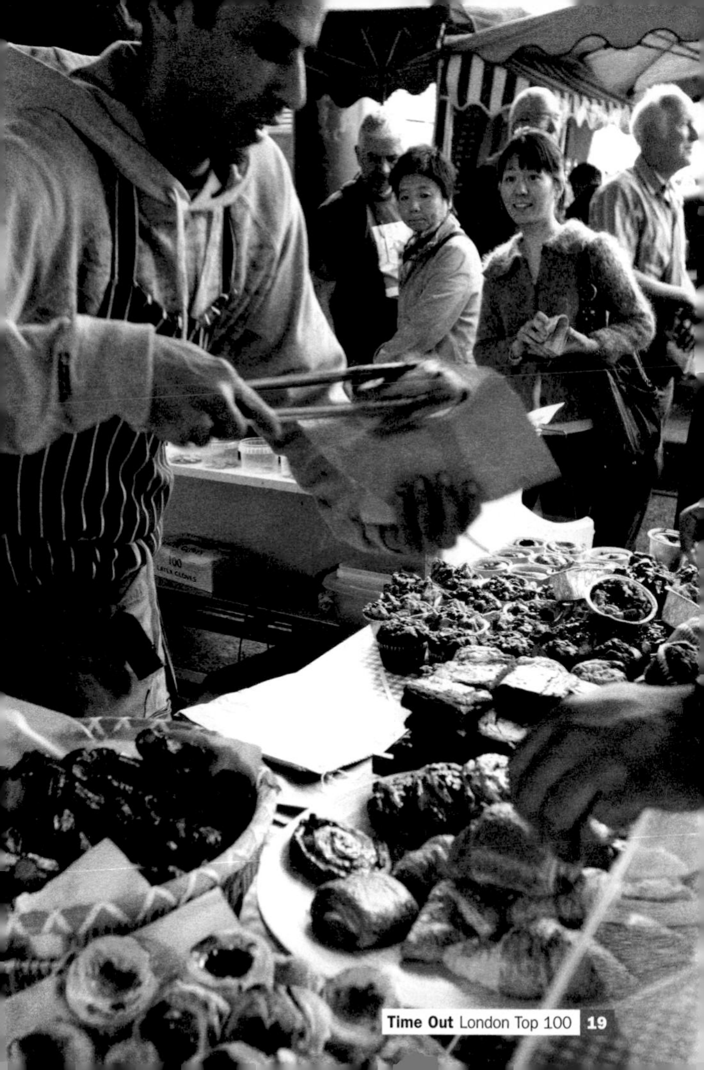

6 Comedy Store

Born during the 1980s 'alternative comedy' boom, the daddy of UK comedy clubs attracts the sharpest, savviest comics on the circuit. For script-free sketches and surreal flights of fancy you can't beat the twice-weekly improvised performances from the resident Comedy Store Players, featuring some of the UK's finest stand-ups. Those who like their comedy with a whiff of terror will relish the King Gong night, on the last Monday of the month, when would-be comics are given as much time on the stage as the rowdy audience will allow – barely time for a one-liner for some sorry souls.

1A Oxendon Street, SW1Y 4EE (0844 847 1728, www.the comedystore.co.uk). Leicester Square or Piccadilly Circus tube.

7 Olympic Park

In a formerly disregarded area of east London, the Olympic Park has unexpectedly become a major tourist attraction, attracting thousands of visitors. There's no public access beyond the perimeter until the 2012 Games begin, but don't worry: it's still fun to check out the various competition venues as they approach completion.

The stars of the show are the round Olympic Stadium and the wave-shaped Aquatics Centre, designed by Zaha Hadid; the impressive Velodrome, shaped like a Pringle crisp, is less visible to the rear of the Park. There are great views from The Greenway, which – along with towpaths beside the River Lea – is a diverting route for an afternoon's walk or cycle ride.

The recycled shipping containers of the View Tube provide all the information you might need about the Park – and, on the ground floor, hot and cold snacks in the busy little Container Café.

The Greenway, Marshgate Lane, E15 2PJ (www.theviewtube.co.uk). Pudding Mill Lane DLR.

8 National Portrait Gallery

The collection at the National Portrait Gallery celebrates the people who have helped to shape British life and culture since the early 16th century – who prove to be a fascinatingly motley crew. Here, you can meet the curious gaze of Sir Winston Churchill, make eyes at rosy-cheeked, saucily attired Nell Gwyn, mistress of Charles II, or watch a sleeping David Beckham, courtesy of artist Sam Taylor-Wood's oddly intimate video installation. The gallery starts with Tudor paintings on the second floor (the Chandos portrait of Shakespeare, Henry VIII by Holbein and the Ditchley Elizabeth I among them); as you approach the present day, the collection starts to include the familiar faces of contemporary sporting heroes, pop stars, actors, writers, politicians and artists. There are sculptures as well as paintings and photographs; in Room 38, you can't miss the bust of Marc Quinn, *Self*, made from the artist's own blood.
St Martin's Place, WC2H 0HE (7306 0055, www.npg.org.uk).
Leicester Square tube or Charing Cross tube/rail.

9 British Museum

Open to 'studious and curious Persons' since it was founded in 1753, this is one of the greatest museums in the world. You could spend days exploring its magnificent collections: highlights include the Parthenon Marbles and Rosetta Stone (left out of the main courtyard, if you enter via the main entrance) and the Egyptian mummies (upstairs, straight ahead). Upstairs, to the right, are the Lindow man, preserved in a peat bog right down to the bristles of his red beard, and the Sutton Hoo treasure hoard. At the museum's heart is the Great Court, now covered by a soaring glass and steel roof, and the circular, dome-topped Reading Room – currently used to house spectacular temporary exhibitions of treasures from around the globe.

Great Russell Street, WC1B 3DG (7323 8299, www.british museum.org). Russell Square or Tottenham Court Road tube.

10 | Wigmore Hall

Superb acoustics and a packed programme (over 400 events are held here each season) mean that the Wigmore, built in 1901, remains the grande dame of London's concert halls. Chamber music is the mainstay, but the Wigmore has moved with the times: pianist Brad Mehldau curates an ongoing series of jazz performances here, and there are all kinds of hands-on workshops and lively special events for small fry.
36 Wigmore Street, W1U 2BP (7935 2141, www.wigmore-hall.org.uk). Bond Street tube.

11 Chelsea Physic Garden

Behind its high brick walls, the Chelsea Physic Garden is an oasis of green that has flourished on this site since 1673. Along with orderly beds of medicinal plants, fragrant lavender and lemon verbena grow in the aromatherapy garden, cacti bristle in the greenhouse, and a lone grapefruit tree flourishes in a sheltered corner. The annual Winter Openings (check the website for dates) showcase a different side of the gardens, with banks of delicate snowdrops lending the place a magical, fairytale feel; afterwards, head to the café for a warming glass of mulled wine and a mince pie.

66 Royal Hospital Road, SW3 4HS (7352 5646, www.chelsea physicgarden.co.uk). Sloane Square tube or bus 11, 19, 239.

While other superclubs have come and gone, the cavernous **Fabric** (77A Charterhouse Street, EC1M 3HN, 7336 8898, www.fabriclondon.com) goes from strength to strength; Friday nights bring the riotously eclectic FabricLive, featuring everyone from Andy C to Simian Mobile Disco, while Saturdays descend into techy, minimal deep house territory. Under the arches of London Bridge, **Cable** (33A Bermondsey Street, SE1 2EG, 7403 7730, www.cable-london.com; pictured above & top right) also has an industrial feel and an impressive line-up on the decks: look out for nights run by the We Fear Silence crew, and Jaded's famed Sunday afterparties.

For more intimate bar-clubs, head out east. In Shoreditch, the two-floor **East Village** (89 Great Eastern Street, EC2A 3HX, 7739 5173, www.eastvillageclub.com; pictured below right) punches well above its weight, boasting the likes of Carl Craig and Derrick Carter on its bill. Meanwhile, some of London's finest promoters mastermind the club nights and gigs at **XOYO** (32-37 Cowper Street, EC2A 4AP, 7490 1198, www.xoyo.co.uk), where sounds run from pop noir to dubstep. Further off the beaten track, **Dalston Superstore** (117 Kingsland High Street, E8 2PB, 7254 2273) is a café by day and a hip and much-hyped gay hangout and club by night, with a NY dive bar vibe and a penchant for electro tunes.

South London has its own small-scale gem in the shape of **Corsica Studios** (4-5 Elephant Road, SE17 1LB, 7703 4760, www.corsica studios.com), whose arty programme embraces poetry, cult bands and genre-defying club nights. Elsewhere in the south, the Vauxhall area is a hedonistic hotspot for gay culture, headed up by the uninhibited, anything-goes **Royal Vauxhall Tavern** (372 Kennington Lane, SE11 5HY, 7820 1222, www.rvt.org.uk; pictured below left) – probably best known for Saturday's exuberant queer performance night, Duckie.

13 Wimbledon

To see the world's leading tennis stars slogging it out on the courts, and indulge in the time-honoured strawberries and cream, Wimbledon (held over two weeks in late June and early July) is the place to be. Unusually for such a major sporting event, you can buy tickets on the day: the All England Club reserves around 500 tickets for Centre Court and No.2 Court at the turnstiles every day from days one to nine of the tournament, while 500 tickets are available over the entire 13 days for No.1 Court. There's plenty of competition for the tickets, so expect to queue from very early in the morning – or even the night before. If you're unsuccessful, several thousand ground admission tickets are also available at the gate daily throughout the tournament, although you don't get access to the show courts. Wimbledon has a big year in 2012: the Olympic Games Tennis competition will be starting here barely a month after the annual Grand Slam tournament ends.

Open year-round, the Wimbledon Lawn Tennis Museum is a sleekly modern affair, where a hologram-like John McEnroe lurks in the 1980s Gentlemen's Dressing Room, reminiscing about old times, and an immersive cinema experience explores the science of the game.

All England Lawn Tennis Club, Church Road, SW19 5AE (8946 6131, www.wimbledon.org). Southfields tube or bus 493.

14 Horniman Museum

Loved by locals (and chosen to symbolise Lewisham on the London 2012 Landmark London pin badges), this one-of-a-kind museum was founded by Victorian tea trader Frederick J Horniman. Egyptian mummies and assorted pickled animals are among the quirky collection of artefacts and specimens from around the globe, along with 1,600 musical instruments; use the touchscreen tables to unleash some weird and wonderful sounds. The basement aquarium, a more recent addition, is divided into seven different zones: look out for the strangely mesmerising moon jellyfish and shoal of British seahorses.

100 London Road, SE23 3PQ (8699 1872, www.horniman.ac.uk). Forest Hill rail or bus 363, 122, 176, 185, P4, P13.

15 | Thames Clippers

As well as carrying suit-clad commuters up and down the Thames, Thames Clippers' fleet of high-speed catamarans (0870 781 5049, www.thamesclippers.com) are a brilliant way to see the sights. Services run all the way from Waterloo Pier, by the London Eye, to Greenwich and Woolwich in the west, with special River Roamer tickets that allow you to hop on and off all day.

▶ *For a scenic return journey to central London, board a Clipper after a gig at the O2 Arena; see no.42.*

16 Kings Place & the new King's Cross

The reinvention of the once-seedy King's Cross neighbourhood continues apace. Since the British Library moved here in the late 1990s, the cavernous Gagosian gallery (6-24 Britannia Street, 7841 9960, www. gagosian.com) has opened, extending US art dealer Larry Gagosian's empire, and St Pancras station was reborn as the Eurostar terminus, combining Victorian grandeur with sleekly modern amenities: a trackside Champagne Bar, restaurants, and assorted shops (among them the London 2012 Shop). A more recent arrival, the Kings Place development is equally slick, with offices (the *Guardian* newspaper is one resident), two art galleries, a restaurant and a café alongside the tranquil canal basin. But it's the basement music facilities that really set Kings Place apart. The acoustically perfect, oak-lined main hall and several smaller spaces are a terrific setting for inventive programming that takes in classical music, jazz, folk, debates and all manner of other delights. Tickets can be very cheap if you book in advance and online.
90 York Way, N1 9AG (0844 264 0321, www.kingsplace.co.uk).
King's Cross tube/rail.

17 London Dungeon

The Victorian railway arches of London Bridge make a suitably spooky location for this gruesome romp through some of the darker episodes in the city's history. The Great Plague, Jack the Ripper, Bloody Mary and a blood-soaked operating theatre are among the attractions: expect a medley of hideous rotting corpses, boils, worm-filled skulls, scuttling rats, piercing screams and all-too-convincing actors, daubed with gore.
28-34 Tooley Street, SE1 2SZ (7403 7221, www.thedungeons.com). London Bridge tube/rail.

Gallery

Studio

18 BFI Southbank

Beside the Thames, tucked underneath Waterloo Bridge, BFI Southbank screens the broadest range of films in London. There are premières, director Q&As, special seasons and interesting programming strands – including the wonderful 'Capital Tales', which focuses on rare London movies. Meanwhile, pre-bookable viewing sessions in the Mediatheque offer the chance to browse the BFI's vast archive, whose treasures run from Edwardian clips of top-hatted gents crossing Blackfriars Bridge to *Monty Python's Flying Circus* and 1950s Morris dancers.

For a larger-than-life cinematic experience and some spectacular 3D screenings, head to the nearby BFI IMAX (1 Charlie Chaplin Walk, SE1 8XR, 7199 6000), whose screen is almost the height of five double-decker buses.

South Bank, SE1 8XT (7928 3535, www.bfi.org.uk). Embankment tube or Waterloo tube/rail.

The shops
Marylebone

...rash, busy Oxford Street, ...one is a polished enclave ...market shops. At its heart is ...ylebone High Street, lined with ...chi boutiques selling everything ...om cool Scandinavian homeware to exquisitely-packaged chocolates and designer clothes. Old-timers and newcomers happily co-exist: at no.83, the Edwardian **Daunt Books** (7224 2295, www.dauntbooks. co.uk; pictured bottom right) is London's loveliest bookshop, with its stained glass windows and old oak galleries, while at no.70, **Apartment C** (7935 1854, www. apartment-c.com) stocks slinky lingerie and serves gin and tonic in china teacups. On Saturday, don't miss the **Cabbages & Frocks** market (www.cabbagesandfrocks.co.uk), which fills the garden of St Marylebone Church with stalls selling vintage clothes, cupcakes and hot food.

Marylebone Lane is also dotted with gems. At **Tracey Neuls**, (no.29, 7935 0039, www.tn29.com; pictured far right), shoes are suspended from the ceiling like artworks, while KJ's Laundry (no.74, 7486 7855, www.kjslaundry.com) wows the fashion crowd with an artful mix of lesser-known talents and established designers. Here, too, is the famous **VV Rouleaux** (no.102, 7224 5179, www.vvrouleaux.com; pictured right) – a treasure trove of ribbons, trims, feathers and butterflies, beloved by fashion stylists. It's impossible to visit without buying a little something: a length of sky-blue velvet ribbon, perhaps, or a tiny silk corsage.

If all that shopping has left you feeling peckish, head back to the High Street and take a left on to Moxon Street – home to two splendid food shops. As well as a stellar selection of cheeses, **La Fromagerie** (nos.2-6, 7935 0341, www.lafromagerie.co.uk) has a fine café, serving charcuterie, cheeses and simple seasonal mains, along with divine cakes and hot chocolate. Alternatively, pop into the **Ginger Pig** (nos.8-10, 7935 7788, www.thegingerpig.co.uk) – one of the capital's finest butchers – for a stupendously good sausage roll.

20 Take afternoon tea

Afternoon tea has long been an institution at the **Ritz** (150 Piccadilly, W1J 9BR, 7493 8181, www.theritzlondon.com; pictured), but now a new generation of establishments are challenging its teatime supremacy – not least the **Wolseley**, a few doors down (160 Piccadilly, W1J 9EB, 7499 6996, www.thewolseley.com). An art deco beauty, it serves lavish stacks of finger sandwiches, scones and cakes; crisp linen, silver teapots and the odd celebrity sighting add to the sense of occasion.

Traditionalists will adore the **Lanesborough** (1 Lanesborough Place, SW1X 7TA, 7259 5599, www.lanesborough.com) on Hyde Park Corner, with its stately decor, toasted teacakes and clotted cream-laden scones; tea is served in silver Russian samovars under the watchful eye of tea sommelier Karl Kessab. For a tea with a more modern twist, try **Espelette** at the Connaught (Carlos Place, W1K 2AL, 3147 7100, www.the-connaught.co.uk), where the tarts, cakes and sandwiches are as deliciously pretty as the surrounds. Subtle updates on the classics are its forte, so wasabi-spiked salmon sandwiches or poppy and strawberry choux might appear alongside more conventional cucumber sarnies and chocolate cake.

Fans of haute couture are advised to take tea in Knightsbridge, in the **Caramel Room** at the Berkeley (Wilton Place, SW1X 7RL, 7235 6000, www.the-berkeley.co.uk). Served on jaunty Paul Smith crockery, its 'Prêt-à-Portea' tea changes every six months in line with the latest collections from the likes of Christopher Kane, Sonia Rykiel and Erdem: you might find yourself biting into a tiny handbag, fashioned from apricot sponge, or a fabulous frock made from macaroons and elderflower gânache.

For an affordable but elegant afternoon tea, head for the **Orangery** (Kensington Palace, Kensington Gardens, W8 4PX, 7376 0239, www.hrp.org.uk). The signature afternoon tea costs under £15 a head – though splashing out a little extra will upgrade you to the champagne version.

21 Whitechapel Gallery

Founded in 1901, this East End gallery has always championed new talent, from Pablo Picasso (*Guernica* was exhibited here in 1939) to Gilbert & George. It still sets its own agenda, with rolling exhibitions that are sometimes offbeat, sometimes risqué, and almost always worth a closer look. Some inspired special events are held here too: an interview with fashion designer Giles Deacon, say, or a free children's illustration workshop led by conceptual artist Jake Chapman. Art aside, the Whitechapel also has a brilliant café-bar and a smart dining room, which has won rave reviews in its own right.

80-82 Whitechapel High Street, E1 7QX (7522 7888, www.whitechapelgallery.org). Aldgate East tube.

22 Hampstead Heath

With its wide open vistas, tangled woodland and undulating hills, Hampstead provides a welcome escape from the city. Picnickers sprawl in the overgrown meadows, dogs bound through the tall grasses with unbridled joy, and exotic-looking fungi lurk amid the trees; happily, the Heath's 800-odd acres are big enough to accommodate all-comers.

Taking a dip in the bathing ponds (Men's, Ladies' and Mixed) is a timeless London experience; while some hardy locals swim year-round, newcomers will find the water bracing, even at the height of summer.

North-west of the ponds, stately **Kenwood House** (8348 1286, www.english-heritage.org.uk) houses a fine collection of paintings and a buzzing self-service café with a sheltered, sun-trap terrace.

Towards the southern edge of the Heath, Parliament Hill offers an extraordinary vista of the city skyline. Its slopes are generally dotted with kite-flyers – and if snow settles in the winter, half of north London turns up to risk life and limb on precarious makeshift sledges. From here, it's an enjoyable stroll into hilly little Hampstead village, with its genteel shops, cafés and restaurants, narrow streets and lovely pubs, including the **Holly Bush** (see no.44).

23 Monument

Designed by Sir Christopher Wren and Robert Hooke as a memorial to the Great Fire of London, the Monument is the world's tallest freestanding stone column. It's an epic 311-step climb up the spiral staircase to the viewing platform: those who make it to the top are rewarded with dizzying views across London, and a certificate. From the ground to the gilded orb that crowns it, the Monument measures 202 feet – the precise distance from its base to Pudding Lane, where the blaze is thought to have started in a bakery on 2 September 1666.

Monument Street, EC3R 8AH (7626 2717, www.themonument.info). Monument tube.

24 All Star Lanes

This is bowling for grown-ups, complete with a s
lit bar with red leather booths and a sleek Ame
you can feast on bourbon-glazed baby back ribs an
sundaes. Score a strike at the original Holborn o
sister establishments in Bayswater and Brick Lan
Victoria House, Bloomsbury Place, WC1B 4DA (
www.allstarlanes.co.uk). Holborn or Russell Squ

Chinatown

North of Leicester Square, a little pocket of central London has been the focus of London's Chinese community since the 1950s (www. chinatownlondon.org). Pagoda-topped phone boxes, Chinese bakeries selling sticky sweets and well-stocked grocery shops give pedestrianised Gerrard Street and the surrounding alleys an exotic feel, and there are a bewildering number of options if you fancy a meal.

Imperial China (White Bear Yard, 25A Lisle Street, WC2H 7BA, 7734 3388, www.imperial-china.co.uk) is more serene than most, entered via a little courtyard complete with wooden footbridge and fishpond, while there's reliably good roast duck at **Four Seasons** (12 Gerrard Street, W1D 5PR, 7494 0870). Chinese students favour the late-opening **HK Diner** (22 Wardour Street, W1D 6QQ, 7434 9544) for bubble tea – a sweet and icy concoction, laced with little balls of tapioca or jelly.

The strong grip that Cantonese restaurants once had on the area is beginning to relax, with more and more establishments offering other regional cuisines. Just beyond Chinatown's borders in Soho, **Barshu** (28 Frith Street, W1D 5LF, 7287 6688, www.bar-shu.co.uk) has been shaking things up with its bold Sichuan flavours, while the Taiwanese dishes at **Leong's Legends** (4 Macclesfield Street, W1D 6AX, 7287 0288; pictured top left) include superb *xiao long bao* – pork or crab dumplings with rich broth sealed inside. Alternatively, sample some terrific Malaysian/ Singaporean street food at the no-frills **Rasa Sayang** (5 Macclesfield Street, W1D 6AY, 7734 1382). New dishes are added regularly, but the excellent *roti canai* (flaky Malaysian flatbread, served with a side of curry) is a fixture among the starters.

To see Chinatown at its most colourful, visit during Chinese New Year in late January or February: scarlet and gold dragons dance through the streets, drums and cymbals noisily ward off evil spirits, and firecrackers pop on the pavement.

DIM SUM
ALL DAY

TAKEAWAY
AVAILABLE

歡迎外

Following the river from its source in the Cotswold Hills, the Thames Path National Trail weaves through central London, hopping from bank to bank. It takes in all kinds of landscapes, from the glorious leafy surrounds of Richmond and Kew to the mini-Manhattan of skyscrapers on the Isle of Dogs. There's even a Victorian foot tunnel under the river from the Isle of Dogs, which pops you up in Greenwich. Good public transport connections and riverboat services make it easy to tackle the walk in sections; for route details and maps, see www.walklondon.org.uk.

For sightseeing and people-watching, you can't beat the stretch along the South Bank from Westminster Bridge to Tower Bridge. It's crammed with London landmarks and cultural big-hitters, from the **London Eye** (see no.49) to **Tate Modern** (see no.75), and has fine views across the water to **Big Ben** (see no.80), **St Paul's** (see no.45) and the **Tower of London** (see no.2). This is also a lively slice of London life. Below the concrete bulk of the **Southbank Centre** (see no.66), skateboarders perfect their kickflips and occasionally come a cropper, while arm-in-arm couples stroll

along the promenade or sip wine at the café-bar in front of **BFI Southbank** (see no.18). Buskers strum guitars, joggers puff past and, by the iconic Oxo Tower, artistic types build sand sculptures on the Thames 'beach'. In summer, with the free Watch This Space festival run by the **National Theatre** (see no.36) in full swing, acrobats, dancers and musicians spill on to the riverside.

As dusk falls, the big sights are illuminated and the lights strung along the riverbanks are reflected in the water: for one of the loveliest views of the city by night, head to Waterloo Bridge.

27 Somerset House

Sandwiched between the grimy, traffic-choked Strand and the River Thames is a broad and calm neoclassical courtyard, with choreographed fountains that children play in all day long if the weather's hot and their parents allow. Effectively a palatial 18th-century office block, Somerset House has cafés (including an expensive one on the Thames-side terrace), a restaurant and the Embankment Galleries, but really comes into its own with a regular programme of seasonal events. For winter, there's the ever-popular outdoor ice-rink; in summer, open-air pop and rock concerts and alfresco film screenings take over the courtyard.

During the day, check out the amazing art in the Courtauld Gallery (7848 2526, www.courtauld.ac.uk/gallery), where admission is free on Monday mornings. Although there are some outstanding early artworks (Cranach's wonderful *Adam & Eve*, for one), the collection's strongest suit is in Impressionist and Post-Impressionist paintings: Manet's *A Bar at the Folies-Bergère*, alongside works by Monet, Cézanne, Gauguin and Van Gogh.

Strand, WC2R 1LA (7845 4600, www.somersethouse.org.uk).
Temple tube or Charing Cross tube/rail.

28 Get pedalling

Short of a brisk walk, a 'Boris Bike' is the cheapest way to get around central London. The chunky blue and silver cycles – affectionately named by locals after Mayor Boris Johnson, who set up the scheme – are picked up from and returned to any of 400 self-service 'docking stations'. Launched in summer 2010, the scheme is geared towards short hops rather than longer loans – and journeys under 30 minutes are free, once you've paid £1 for 24 hours' access.

The bikes feature a bell, pedal-powered lights and a rack with an elastic cord with which to secure your possessions – though if you want to wear a cycle helmet, you'll need to bring your own.

You can become a member of the scheme and get your own 'key' by signing up on the Transport for London website. Alternatively, casual users can register for temporary access, either online, by phone or by using the credit-card readers at docking stations. For more information on the scheme, visit www.tfl.gov.uk.

29 Topshop

Over 200,000 shoppers enter the hallowed portals of Topshop's immense flagship store every week. Canny collaborations with famous designers (from Biba's Barbara Hulanicki to fashionista favourite Christopher Kane) and hotly tipped young graduates have rocketed it to the front of the fashion pack, and into the wardrobe of many a bargain-loving celebrity.
214 Oxford Street, W1W 8LG (0844 848 7487, www.topshop.com). Oxford Circus tube.

30 Royal Albert Hall & the Proms

Resplendent in red brick, this vast Victorian concert venue is a superb setting for the BBC Sir Henry Wood Promenade Concerts, better known as the Proms (0845 401 5040, www.bbc.co.uk/proms). Held between mid July and mid September, the Proms include around 70 concerts, running from early music recitals to orchestral world premières. You can book ahead, but £5 'promenade' tickets are available if you queue on the day, giving access to the standing-room stalls or the gallery at the very top of the auditorium. For the rest of the year, the programme mixes classical concerts with rock and pop acts, with elaborate ballet performances and carol singalongs at Christmas.

Kensington Gore, SW7 2AP (7589 3203 information, 7589 8212 tickets, www.royalalberthall.com). South Kensington tube or bus 9, 10, 52, 452.

The restaurant that jump-started the trend for Modern British food was **St John** (26 St John Street, EC1M 4AY, 7251 0848, www.stjohn restaurant.com). Set near Smithfield meat market, it is famed for chef Fergus Henderson's 'nose to tail' eating ethos, with offal, bone marrow and unfamiliar bits of beast often featured on the menu. Lambs' tongues and tripe aren't for everyone, though, and the seasonally focused menu also caters to more squeamish souls with the likes of brill with fennel and green sauce, creamy cauliflower soup and good old-fashioned desserts: bread and butter pudding, for instance, or steamed date sponge with butterscotch sauce.

Newer on the scene is Soho's **Hix** (66-70 Brewer Street, W1F 9UP, 7292 3518, www.hixsoho.co.uk; pictured above), a showcase for Mark Hix's considerable culinary talents. Native oysters, roast grouse and hangar steak are regulars on the menu. Before dinner, head down to the basement for a precision-mixed cocktail in Mark's Bar.

Superb British produce, cooked with a minimum of fuss, is the mainstay at busy little **Hereford Road** (3 Hereford Road, W2 4AB, 7727 1144, www.herefordroad.org) in Bayswater. Dishes such as potted crab or partridge with lentils, savoy cabbage and bacon are as simple as they are satisfying. Save room for the magnificent desserts.

The informal and inexpensive **Albion at the Boundary Project** (2-4 Boundary Street, E2 7DD, 7729 1051, www.albioncaff.co.uk; pictured below) is part of an East End Victorian warehouse conversion that also contains a more formal restaurant, boutique hotel rooms and a rooftop bar. It's open all day, serving sturdy British grub: kipper or bacon and eggs for breakfast, say, then fish and chips, steak and kidney pudding or juicy portobello mushrooms on toast for lunch or dinner.

For British ales and classic cooking, Greenwich's **Old Brewery** (Pepys Building, Old Royal Naval College, SE10 9LW, 3327 1280, www.old brewerygreenwich.com) is a good bet. A convivial café by day and a restaurant by night, its main dining room has a display of gleaming copper tuns; if that gives you a thirst, there are around 50 beers on the menu.

▶ *London's laidback gastropubs also offer some fine Modern British cooking;* *see no.85.*

No.31 Lincoln's Inn Fields was home to Georgian architect Sir John Soane – and having become a museum after his death in 1837, its wonderful eccentricity remains perfectly preserved. A quite extraordinary array of art and antiquities fills every nook and cranny of the labyrinthine interior, taking in Grecian sculptures, crumbling architectural fragments and assorted busts, bronzes and curiosities. The Picture Room is crammed with treasures, some of which are hidden away in ingenious fold-out panels; in pride of place is Hogarth's *A Rake's Progress*, whose eight paintings chart the downfall of a spendthrift young dandy. Downstairs are the death masks and stately funerary urns of the Crypt Room, whose centrepiece is a huge Egyptian sarcophagus, carved from a single piece of alabaster.

Here, too, is the parlour Soane designed for Padre Giovanni, an entirely imaginary monk; the good Padre's 'tomb' – which in fact houses the remains of Soane's lap dog, Fanny – is out in the courtyard. The candlelit tours held on the first Tuesday of the month are a brilliantly atmospheric way to appreciate the museum, though be prepared to queue.

31 Lincoln's Inn Fields, WC2A 3BP (7405 2107, www.soane. org). Holborn tube.

Costing £20 million and taking five years to build, the lower-ground-floor Galleries of Modern London were a thrilling addition to the superb Museum of London when they opened in spring 2010. Telling the city's story from the Great Fire in 1666 to the present day, the space is packed with intriguing artefacts and engaging interactives.

Highlights include a recreated Georgian pleasure garden, whose mannequins sport historic dresses matched with contemporary Philip Treacy masks and hats; an actual 18th-century debtor's prison cell, with graffiti still clearly legible; and the Lord Mayor's dazzling gold coach, which is wheeled out of the gallery each November for a starring role in the Lord Mayor's Show (see no.39). Upstairs, meanwhile, you can see a reconstructed Roman dining room and the huge bone of an aurochs.

By far the most moving exhibit, though, is the Blitz gallery. Beneath an unexploded World War II bomb, starkly suspended from the ceiling in a glass case, runs the heart-rending but often surprisingly good-humoured testimony of ordinary survivors of the German bombs, bringing Londoners' famous 'Blitz Spirit' to life.

150 London Wall, EC2Y 5HN (0870 444 3851, www.museum oflondon.org.uk). Barbican or St Paul's tube.

Dulwich Picture Gallery

This diminutive gallery makes for a fine afternoon's excursion, punching well above its weight with its collection of Old Masters. Works by Rembrandt, Rubens and Gainsborough are among those showcased in the quietly dignified neoclassical premises, built in 1811 by Sir John Soane. After admiring the paintings, check out the curious lighting effects in the mausoleum (built by Soane for the gallery's founders) then stop for lunch in the elegant, airy little café.

Gallery Road, SE21 7AD (8693 5254, www.dulwichpicturegallery.org.uk). North Dulwich or West Dulwich rail.

erating Theatre, um & Herb Garret

Atmosphere is everything at this little museum. Up a steep spiral staircase are cases of brutal old surgical tools, bunches of herbs and unmentionable things in jars. The star of the show, however, is a pre-anaesthetic operating theatre with tiered viewing seats for students, which dates from 1822. Book ahead for one of the brilliantly convincing surgical re-enactments – if you've got a strong stomach.

9A St Thomas's Street, SE1 9RY (7188 2679, www.thegarret. org.uk). London Bridge tube/rail.

36 National Thea

As you'd expect, the NT stages plenty of s
auditoriums, featuring a stellar cast
Shakespearean tragedies share the bill w
classics and all manner of new produ
experimental pieces to the big-budget likes
impeccable artistic credentials, the National
with free early-evening concerts in the foyer ta
stamping flamenco to boogie-woogie piano, an
and theatre skills workshops. Best of all is the
which runs from June to September. Covered   ...en AstroTurf, the
outdoor Theatre Square becomes an alfresco stage for tightrope-walkers,
puppeteers, tango dancers and madcap tea parties; events are free, so
simply turn up and see what's on.
*South Bank, SE1 9PX (7452 3400 information, 7452 3000 tickets,
www.nationaltheatre.org.uk). Embankment or Southwark tube, or
Waterloo tube/rail.*

Camden Market

Culture and commerce meet at Camden Market, which is at its best at the weekend. Trousers bristling with spikes, neon tutus and army fatigues are among the goods, along with battered cowboy boots, swirly 1970s frocks and arty-crafty accessories. You'll see more mohicans here than anywhere else in London, while lashings of black eyeliner are an essential for the teenagers who loiter beside the Lock.

The market's various subsections sprawl north from Camden Town tube, with tentacles reaching out alongside the canal, up Inverness Street, around Camden Lock (head to the West Yard for the best food stalls), into Stables Market (known for its vintage dealers) and the Horse Hospital. On Sunday afternoons, Camden Town tube is exit-only: catch a bus or walk north beyond the market to Chalk Farm station.

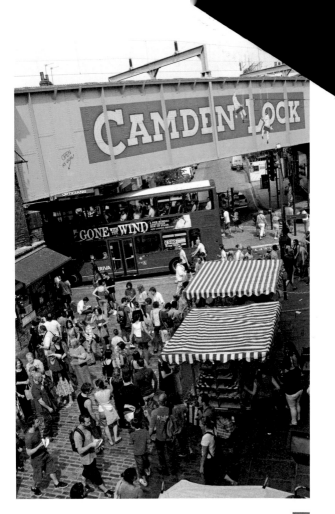

...ngton Palace

...packs a lot of history into a relatively small red-brick
...505, the original merchant's house was expanded by
...en after William III and Mary II bought the place in 1689,
...ng found the air more congenial than on damp, polluted
...en Victoria was born in the palace in 1819, and it was
he... ..., that the formerly carefree young princess learnt that the
death o... ...er uncle, William IV, had made her queen. More recently, in
1997, the funeral procession for Diana, Princess of Wales, set off from
Kensington Palace.

Until restoration work is completed in 2012, only the State Apartments
are open to the public, housing the theatrical 'Enchanted Palace'
exhibition. It tells the tragic stories of seven of the palace's princesses,
with installations, performance and interactives built around the Royal
Ceremonial Dress Collection, and spectacular special commissions from
star fashion designers such as Vivienne Westwood.

***Kensington Gardens, W8 4PX (0844 482 7777, www.hrp.org.uk).
High Street Kensington or Queensway tube.***

▶ *If you fancy taking tea, the formal Sunken Garden is a beautiful
setting for the opulent Orangery café; see no.20.*

39 Fireworks

Londoners have always loved fireworks – after all, as far back as 1749 Handel had composed music to accompany a display in Green Park. Nowadays, some of the most spectacular displays explode over the Thames, with the city's cluster of central bridges providing superb vantage points.

Autumn is the peak season: the **Mayor's Thames Festival** (7928 8998, www.thamesfestival.org) in early September and the **Lord Mayor's Show** (7332 3456, www. lordmayorsshow.org) in early November both close with an impressive bang, while the handy confluence of Diwali (the Hindu Festival of Light) and Bonfire Night (the traditional commemoration of Guy Fawkes' 1605 failure to blow up the Houses of Parliament) makes the weekend nearest to the **Fifth of November** a feast of fiery fun. Battersea Park, Clapham Common, Ravenscourt Park and Victoria Park usually have enormous bonfires and some spectacular fireworks, but you could also pre-book a late ride on the **London Eye** (see no.49) to see displays blooming all over town.

Walkways lead past the Barbican Estate's rectangular ponds and artistically angular towers of flats to reach Europe's largest multi-arts centre, set by a central lakeside terrace. Its programming is brilliantly varied, taking in gigs by cult rock stars, concerts from the resident London Symphony Orchestra, flying visits from international dance companies and inspired film screenings, from classic Hitchcock to Japanese horror. Exhibitions are equally bold, with a heady blend of architecture, fashion, art and design, and there are regular tours of the estate itself – a landmark of Modernist architecture.

Silk Street, EC2Y 8DS (7638 4141, www.barbican.org.uk).
Barbican tube or Moorgate tube/rail.

41 Fortnum & Mason

This plush temple to fine foods, teas and wine is in good fettle after a 300th birthday revamp. Its premises on Piccadilly ooze understated luxury: even the rooftop beehives, which supply the store's own-brand honey, are palatial affairs, painted in Fortnum's signature shade of blue-green eau-de-Nil. Goods range from truffles to terrines (not forgetting the famous hampers), and there are five impressive restaurants; in the plush 1707 Wine Bar, you can sip a bottle of your choice from the excellent wine department on payment of a £10 corkage fee.

181 Piccadilly, W1A 1ER (7734 8040, www.fortnumandmason. co.uk). Green Park or Piccadilly Circus tube.

42 O2 Arena/North Greenwich Arena

Standing in solitary splendour on the tip of the Greenwich peninsula, the dome of this huge arena, with its 12 yellow masts, has become a modern London landmark. Originally built to mark the millennium, the vast space has been reinvented as a multi-talented venue – host to spectacular gigs (everyone from the Scissor Sisters to Shakira) and blockbuster sporting events. Towering talents from the NBA, beefy WWE wrestlers and top-seeded tennis players have all battled it out in front of the crowds here, and it is the chosen venue (as the North Greenwich Arena) for several high-profile London 2012 competitions: Basketball, Wheelchair Basketball, Artistic Gymnastics and Trampoline Gymnastics.

The complex also takes in the smaller IndigO2 venue, interactive pop-music museum the British Music Experience (8463 2000, www.british musicexperience.com), a multiplex with one super-sized screen and lots of restaurants and cafés.

Millennium Way, SE10 0BB (8463 2000 information, 0844 856 0202 tickets, www.theo2.co.uk). North Greenwich tube.
▶ *The most scenic way to get to and from the arena is by river, aboard a Thames Clipper; see no.15.*

43 Wallace Collection

Discreetly located on a quiet Marylebone square, the Wallace is a delight. The galleries are an unusual combination of arms and armour, furniture, porcelain and glassware, sculpture and exquisite objets d'art, but the real thrill is seeing artistic masterpieces in a relaxed townhouse setting. 'Masterpieces' is no exaggeration: paintings by Gainsborough, Poussin, Rembrandt, Titian and Velázquez are on display here, as is Frans Hals' *Laughing Cavalier*. Admission is free.

Hertford House, Manchester Square, W1U 3BN (7935 0687, www.wallacecollection.org). Bond Street tube.

44 Have a pint

Gastropubs and slick cocktail bars are all very well, but sometimes all you want is a decent pint in a friendly, old-fashioned boozer. For sheer Victorian splendour, the **Princess Louise** (208-209 High Holborn, WC1V 7BW, 7405 8816; pictured top left, top right & bottom right) in Holborn is unrivalled. Its darkly cosy, wood-panelled interior, stucco ceiling and intricate etched glass are wonderfully grand – but as it's a Samuel Smith's pub, beer is refreshingly cheap. A 15-minute walk away, just off Hatton Garden, the tiny, oak-fronted **Ye Olde Mitre** (1 Ely Court, Ely Place, EC1N 6SJ, 7405 4751) offers a more intimate drinking experience. Notoriously tricky to find, it's open weekdays only; those that do stumble on it are rewarded by well-kept real ales and delightfully crooked, cramped surrounds.

Another diminutive gem is the **Lamb & Flag** (33 Rose Street, WC2E 9EB, 7497 9504), squirrelled away down an alley in the heart of Covent Garden. Two centuries' worth of cuttings and caricatures adorn the walls, while ploughman's lunches and scotch eggs are among the classic pub grub on offer; come in the afternoon to avoid the after-work rush. On summer evenings, crowds spill into the streets, while the fire emits a hospitable glow on chilly winter days. Up in Hampstead, the **Holly Bush** (22 Holly Mount, NW3 6SG, 7435 2892; pictured bottom left) is another old-fashioned boozer with a welcoming fire in the grate. It's a low-ceilinged, inviting place with cask ales and battered oak settles – ideal after a walk across the Heath.

In summer, the great British beer garden comes into its own – and one of the nicest spots for an alfresco pint is the tranquil walled terrace at the **Albion** (10 Thornhill Road, N1 1HW, 7607 7450, www.the-albion. co.uk), a polished-up Georgian beauty in Islington that's known for its superior Sunday roasts. Its wisteria-entwined pergola, wooden tables and herb garden ooze rustic charm.

If you'd prefer a view over the Thames, follow in the footsteps of Graham Greene, Dylan Thomas and Ernest Hemingway and head for the **Dove** (19 Upper Mall, W6 9TA, 8748 9474) in Hammersmith. The 17th-century beamed interior is full of character, but on sunny days the best seats in the house are on the little Thames-side terrace.

45 St Paul's Cathedral

Over the last decade, a £40m restoration project has removed much of the Victorian grime from Sir Christopher Wren's cathedral, and the façade looks as bright as it must have done when the last stone was placed in 1708. Up in the Whispering Gallery, the acoustics are so good that a whisper can carry to the opposite side of the dome; keep on climbing to the exterior Golden Gallery for spectacular City views. If the steps are too much, head down into the maze-like crypt; here, in addition to Nelson's grand tomb and Wren's small, plain memorial, you'll find a 270° film that recounts the cathedral's history and flies you to the top of the dome.
Ludgate Hill, EC4M 8AD (7246 8357, www.stpauls.co.uk).
St Paul's tube.

46 Science Museum

The sheer scale of the Science Museum is impressive. Straight after the bag check, you're confronted by enormous 18th-century steam engines in the Energy Hall, while rockets are suspended from the ceiling in the 'Exploring Space' gallery. Alongside the Apollo 10 capsule, displays explain how astronauts eat, sleep and go to the loo in space. There are more iconic objects in 'Making the Modern World', ranging from Stephenson's *Rocket* locomotive to a chunky 1980s mobile phone. Four further floors explore computing, flight, mathematics, medicine and astronomy, with child-friendly pulleys, explosions and other interactive experiments in the third-floor Launchpad gallery.

Bathed in an eerie blue light, the Wellcome Wing is where the museum ensures it stays on the cutting edge, from looking at breaking science news to investigating climate change. Don't miss the futuristic-looking silver pods in 'Who Am I?', where you can find out what gender your brain is, see what you'll look like in ten years' time, and discover what makes you unique – if you can get past the crowds of eager children, that is.

Admission to the permanent collections is free, though some of the more exotic interactives – the 'Legend of Apollo' 4-D space trip, the 'Fly Zone' flight simulation, films in the IMAX cinema – do cost extra. **Exhibition Road, SW7 2DD (7942 4000 switchboard, 0870 870 4868 information, www.sciencemuseum.org.uk). South Kensington tube.**

▶ *South Kensington's famous trio of Victorian museums also includes the V&A (see no.3) and the Natural History Museum (see no.83).*

47 Spitalfields & Brick Lane

Tucked into the shadows of the City's skyscrapers, the area around Spitalfields and Brick Lane is perfect for a leisurely Sunday browse, with offbeat shops, market stalls, street eats and cafés.

The days of wholesale fruit and veg are long gone at the Victorian **Old Spitalfields Market** (7247 8556, www.oldspitalfieldsmarket.com; pictured). Instead, expect an arty array of hand-printed T-shirts, vintage frocks, bric-a-brac and food stalls, surrounded by a sleek shopping precinct. Although the market is open on weekdays, Sundays are busiest and best: come with spending money, as cashpoints are in short supply.

Next, press on to the **Sunday (Up)Market** (www.sundayupmarket.co.uk) in the nearby Truman Brewery, which has a crafty fashion vibe all its own. Homespun food stalls sell everything from thalis to tapas, and there are plenty of quirky clothes, gifts and accessories being sold by fresh-faced young designers.

Truman Brewery yard opens on to **Brick Lane** (www.visitbricklane.org), lined with Bangladeshi cafés, curry houses and sari shops, along with quirky boutiques and vintage emporiums. For the coolest cluster of shops in the neighbourhood, head north up Brick Lane towards Bethnal Green then turn right on to Cheshire Street: highlights include the chic leather satchels and purses at **Mimi** (no.40, 7729 6699, www.mimiberry.co.uk) and the gorgeous homeware, prints and trinkets at **Shelf** (no.40, 7739 9444, www.helpyourshelf.co.uk).

48 WWT London Wetland Centre

A mere four miles from central London, this 104-acre nature reserve feels half a world away. The tranquil ponds, rustling reedbeds and wildflower meadows teem with bird life – some 150 species in all – as well as the now-rare water vole. Bats are accommodated in style at the architect-designed Berkeley Bat House, with its stark white lines and intricate façade.

Queen Elizabeth's Walk, SW13 9WT (8409 4400, www.wwt. org.uk). Hammersmith tube then bus 283, Barnes rail or bus 33, 72, 209.

49 London Eye

For unrivalled views across the city, head 44
in one of the London Eye's glass pods. The
travel the 1,392-foot circumference (424 met
the top – if the weather's clear – you can see
some 25 miles away.
Jubilee Gardens, SE1 7PB (0870 500 0600, w
Westminster tube or Waterloo tube/rail.

wer Bridge

stinctive that Nazi bombers used it as a navigation aid during the itz, Tower Bridge has a drawbridge design that allows big ships to pass through. It still regularly raises its double bascules (now powered by electricity rather than steam), sometimes several times a day. To see it in action, consult the website for scheduled times over the next three days, or follow the Twitter updates (http://twitter.com/towerbridge). Visit the exhibition and you can take in the view from one of the high-level walkways that connect the two spiky towers, and explore the engine rooms.

Tower Bridge Exhibition, Tower Bridge, SE1 2UP (7403 3761, www.towerbridge.org.uk). Tower Hill tube or Tower Gateway DLR.

51 Museum of London Docklands

A lofty Georgian warehouse accommodates this huge museum, which explores the history of London's docklands and the River Thames. In the Sailortown gallery, you can wander a re-creation of the narrow streets of Wapping as they were some 150 years ago, complete with the sound of drunken sailors and a wild animal emporium. Other exhibitions carry a real emotional charge – not least the London, Sugar & Slavery exhibition, which explores the city's involvement in the transatlantic slave trade. *No.1 Warehouse, West India Quay, Hertsmere Road, E14 4AL (7001 9844, www.museumindocklands.org.uk). Canary Wharf tube or West India Quay DLR.*

52 HMS Belfast

Now a floating outpost of the Imperial War Museum, this 11,500-tonne battlecruiser is the last surviving big-gun World War II warship in Europe, and played a key role in the D-Day landings. Excited children dart up the steep, narrow ladders and tear around her gun turrets, bridge, decks and engine room, while a free audio guide reveals what life was like on board (decidedly cramped, with up to 950 sailors in residence).
Morgan's Lane, Tooley Street, SE1 2JH (7940 6300, www.iwm.org.uk). London Bridge tube/rail.

53 Hyde Park & Kensington Gardens

Occupying a 350-acre slice of central London, **Hyde Park** (7298 2000, www.royalparks.org.uk) has a long and varied history. In the 18th century, the smart set trotted along Rotten Row on horseback; in June 1908, 250,000 suffragettes shocked polite society when they gathered here to demand votes for women. Marches and protests still take place in the park, and on Sunday mornings all sorts of people clamber on boxes to exercise their freedom of speech at Speakers' Corner, as they have done since 1872; some are less than coherent, but the heckling and banter is always entertaining.

The lower end of the park is given over to the waterfowl and boats of the Serpentine, with little pedalos and rowing boats for hire from Easter to October. This is where the Swimming Marathon and the Swimming segment of the Triathlon will be held during the London 2012 Games; you can test the water temperature for yourself by swimming in the roped-off lido, alongside the ducks. To the south of the Serpentine, by the lido, the Diana, Princess of Wales Memorial Fountain is a calming, gently curving channel made from smooth Cornish granite.

To the east, the lovely **Kensington Gardens** take in stately Italian gardens, avenues of trees and the famous bronze statue of Peter Pan beside the Long Water. The superb Diana Memorial Playground is also Peter Pan-themed, with a resplendent wooden pirate ship at its centre. Art lovers will enjoy the small but inventive **Serpentine Gallery** (7402 6075, www.serpentinegallery.org), which hosts modern and contemporary art exhibitions. Afterwards, stroll across to Sir George Gilbert Scott's extravagant Albert Memorial – Victorian pomp and splendour at its most gloriously overblown.

▶ *From here, it's the shortest of strolls to Kensington Palace, at the western end of Kensington Gardens; see no.38.*

54 Geffrye Museum

Peek into Londoners' living rooms at this delightful museum, a converted set of 18th-century almshouses. The recreated rooms skip through the centuries, from 1600 to the present day, and there are changing temporary exhibitions; the 'Stories of the World' strand, in association with the London 2012 Cultural Olympiad, will investigate the influences from other cultures that have helped shape English homes. The pleasure of exploring this collection is in the details (a bell jar of stuffed birds, perhaps, or a 1960s bubble TV). Pretty gardens are hidden at the rear. *136 Kingsland Road, E2 8EA (7739 9893, www.geffrye-museum. org.uk). Hoxton rail.*

Covering a 43-acre site, Westfield offers retail therapy on a grand scale. Its 265 shops run from retail giants to such intimate boutiques as denim specialist Donna Ida or slinky lingerie label Myla, while the presence of fashion big-hitters including Vuitton, Burberry and Prada adds an haute-couture edge to proceedings. A host of cafés and restaurants revive footsore shoppers, and solicitous concierges smooth the way to consumer nirvana with a raft of extra services, from valet parking to 'handsfree' shopping – some free, some not. Due to open in autumn 2011 alongside the London 2012 Olympic Park, the new Westfield Stratford City will be bigger and promises to be even better: brace your bank account.

Ariel Way, W12 7GF (3371 2300, http://uk.westfield.com/london).
White City or Wood Lane tube, or Shepherd's Bush tube/rail.

56 Saunter through Soho

Although the seedy Soho of gangsters, pimps and strip clubs is nowadays mostly consigned to black-and-white photographs, this is still a lively area to visit. Much of the daytime action happens along Old Compton Street – a gay-friendly superhighway of streetside cafés, among them the open-all-hours 1950s caff **Bar Italia** (22 Frith Street, W1D 4RP, 7437 4520, www.baritaliasoho.co.uk) – or else among the loungers and layabouts who populate the four little lawns of Soho Square at the first hint of sunshine. Berwick Street, with its rough-and-tumble fruit market, second-hand vinyl shops and high-design dim sum teahouse, **Yauatcha** (15 Broadwick Street, W1F 0DL, 7494 8888, www.yauatcha.com), gives an appropriately jumbled flavour of modern Soho.

With the sex trade retreating to a few dark corners (peep shows linger at Tisbury Court and the eastern end of Brewer Street), the prevailing Soho industries are media-related. Meanwhile, west Soho has remodelled itself as a shopping destination, with Carnaby Street and the surrounding alleys increasingly home to the kind of chic boutiques that were common in its swinging '60s heyday.

The need to feed the media crowd has created such superb restaurants as **Arbutus** and **Hix** (for both, see no.31), while sparsely modern cafés such as **Fernandez & Wells** (73 Beak Street, W1F 9SR, 7287 8124, www.fernandezandwells.com) and the fiercely coffee-focused **Milk Bar** (3 Bateman Street, W1D 4AG, 7287 4796) compete with the more traditional likes of **Maison Bertaux** (28 Greek Street, W1D 5DQ, 7437 6007, www.maisonbertaux.com; pictured top right), with its oozing eclairs and wonderfully light choux pastries.

If you're feeling louche and thirsty, quaff a cider at Francis Bacon's local, the **French House** (49 Dean Street, W1D 5BG, 7437 2799, www.frenchhousesoho.com), or a cocktail at the stylish, dimly lit **Milk & Honey** (61 Poland Street, W1F 7NU, 7065 6841, www.mlkhny.com) – open to non-members before 11pm, if you call ahead.

57 Royal Botanic Ga[...] (Kew Gardens)

Kew's 300 acres take in a spectacular array of plan[...]
monsters on the lookout for passing insects to centur[...]
nothing quite like wandering among the verdant foliage [...]
in the humid Palm House on a cold winter's day; come [...]
of purple and white crocuses is one of the first signs of s[...] leafy,
lofty perspective on the gardens, stroll through the treeto[...] on the Xstrata
Treetop Walkway, some 60 feet (18 metres) above ground.

Kew, Richmond, Surrey TW9 3AB (8332 5655, www.kew.org).
Kew Gardens tube/rail, Kew Bridge rail or riverboat to Kew Pier.

ational Gallery

e National contains a bewildering number of must-see paintings from the world's finest artists – Cézanne's *Bathers*, one of the *Sunflowers* paintings by Van Gogh, Constable's *The Hay Wain* and *The Madonna of the Pinks* by Raphael among them. If you're not sure where to start, use the ArtStart touchscreens in the Sainsbury Wing and the East Wing Espresso Bar to choose a themed tour or plot your own course through the highlights (you can print your route for free). Also in the Sainsbury Wing, there's great artistry in the cooking at the National Dining Rooms (the attached bakery-café is a cheaper option), while the East Wing contains the darkly handsome – and late-opening – National Café.

Trafalgar Square, WC2N 5DN (7747 2885, www.nationalgallery. org.uk). Leicester Square tube or Charing Cross tube/rail.

65

59 Eat well for less

The capital has its fair share of pricey fine dining restaurants, but you don't have to spend a fortune to eat well here. The two-course set lunch at **Pied à Terre** (34 Charlotte Street, W1T 2NH, 7636 1178, www.pied-a-terre. co.uk; pictured near right) is one of the best bargains in town, at £23.50 (canapés included). The dining room may be slightly austere, but Michelin-starred chef Shane Osborn assembles his dishes with the eye of an artist, often including tiny edible flowers or herbs picked from the little rooftop garden.

Alternatively, try the set lunch menu at **Launceston Place** (1A Launceston Place, W8 5RL, 7937 6912, www.danddlondon.com) – a mere £20 for three courses. The food is Modern British (duck egg on toast with Somerset truffle, say, followed by Denham Castle lamb and pommes purée), the interior moodily cosy, and the desserts a triumph. The lunch and pre- and post-theatre menu at **Arbutus** (63-64 Frith Street, W1D 3JW, 7734 4545, www.arbutus restaurant.co.uk; pictured bottom left) is another three-course triumph for under £20. If it's on the menu, finish with the floating island: luscious, vanilla-flecked custard topped with fluffy meringue.

You can even take set menus out of the equation by heading for **Zucca** (184 Bermondsey Street, SE1 3TQ, 7378 6809, www.zuccalondon.com; pictured top right), near London Bridge. A modern, open-plan establishment, it serves simple but beautifully executed Italian food: tagliatelle with artichokes and lemon, perhaps, or sage- and garlic-spiked braised pork with polenta.

In the centre of Soho, the small but splendid **Giaconda Dining Room** (9 Denmark Street, WC2H 8LS, 7240 3334, www.giacondadining.com; pictured top left and bottom right) also offers polished fare at very reasonable prices. Expect an inviting, bistro-style menu: crispy duck confit is always a good bet, along with the hearty grill of the day with braised shallots and chips.

60 Westminster Cathedral

The most important Catholic church in England is a somewhat surprising sight among the office blocks of Victoria. With its Byzantine domes, arches and soaring tower, it would look more at home in the middle of Istanbul. No wonder: architect John Francis Bentley, who built it between 1895 and 1903, was heavily influenced by the Hagia Sophia. The interior is richly adorned with mosaics and marble, while 'Treasures of the Cathedral' displays an impressive Arts & Crafts coronet, a Tudor chalice, holy relics and Bentley's amazing architectural model of his cathedral, complete with tiny hawks. A lift runs 273 feet (83 metres) up the bell tower for great views over this historic district.

42 Francis Street, SW1P 1QW (7798 9055, www.westminster cathedral.org.uk). Victoria tube/rail.

Experience theatre Elizabethan-style at this oak[...] of the Globe Theatre (the original, co-owned by [...] burned to the ground in 1613). That means open[...] hard wooden benches; paying a little extra to rent[...] well spent. It's standing-room only if you're a 'groun[...] mere £5 a ticket, and thrillingly close to the onstage [...] *21 New Globe Walk, Bankside, SE1 9DT (7401 99[...] www.shakespeares-globe.org). Southwark tube or L[...] Bridge tube/rail.*

...de the Routemaster

London's classic double-deckers were withdrawn from general service in 2005, but beautifully refurbished Routemasters still run a couple of shortened routes. The no.9 (Stop B) and no.15 (Stop S) depart from Cockspur Street, at the south-west corner of Trafalgar Square, every 15 minutes from 9.30am to 6.30pm. The no.9 bus potters west to the Royal Albert Hall, and is handy for the South Kensington museums; the no.15 goes east through the City to the Tower of London, via St Paul's Cathedral. The buses accept regular tickets and Travelcards, but you must buy them before boarding the bus.

63 City Farms

For a slice of country life in the midst of the city, check out one of London's many city farms. The biggest is **Mudchute Park & Farm** (Pier Street, Isle of Dogs, E14 3HP, 7515 5901, www.mudchute.org), where you can stand in a meadow full of grazing sheep while taking in the soaring skyscrapers of Canary Wharf. Mild-eyed cows, inquisitive llamas and sprightly Indian Runner ducks are among the residents, along with cuddly beasties for children to pet: after meeting the animals, refuel at the Mudchute Kitchen. Another favourite is **Hackney City Farm** (1A Goldsmiths Row, E2 8QA, 7729 6381, www.hackneycityfarm.co.uk; pictured), where Bella the saddleback pig rules the farmyard. In spring you might meet a wobbly-legged newborn lamb, and there are always rabbits, chinchillas and guinea pigs to coo over. Stop for lunch at the superb Frizzante Café, then head home with a box of freshly laid eggs. In south London, **Crystal Palace Park Farm** (The Croft, Ledrington Road, SE19 2BS, 8778 5572, www.crystalpalaceparkfarm.co.uk) has paddocks and a small yard, as well as lovely views. Along with the usual small furries, there are Shetland ponies, kune pigs, goats, alpacas and reptiles. The farm has no café, but the surrounding parkland is great for picnics.

For a full list of city farms, consult the **Federation of City Farms and Community Gardens** (0117 923 1800, www.farmgarden.org.uk).

64 Imperial War Museum

The IWM's imposing premises were once a notorious lunatic asylum (the Bethlehem Royal Hospital, aka Bedlam). Nowadays the main hall is occupied by the machinery of war: antique guns, tanks, aircraft and artillery. The two World Wars are covered in depth, while the Holocaust Exhibition (not recommended for under-14s) traces the history of European anti-Semitism and its nadir in the concentration camps. On the top floor, Crimes Against Humanity (unsuitable for under-16s) looks at contemporary genocide and ethnic conflict. The new Lord Ashcroft Gallery houses the Extraordinary Heroes exhibition, recounting the tales of bravery and gallantry that lie behind the world's largest collection of Victoria and George Crosses.

Lambeth Road, SE1 6HZ (7416 5320, www.iwm.org.uk).
Lambeth North tube or Elephant & Castle tube/rail.

65 Wembley Stadium

For football fans, the new Wembley Stadium is no less a shrine than its predecessor, no matter that the iconic twin towers have given way to architecture supremo Lord Foster's landmark leaning arch. Highlights of a tour include sitting in the manager's dug-out and the home dressing room, and climbing the Trophy Winners' steps to the Royal Box, where you get to lay a hand on a (very valuable) replica of the FA Cup. The principal venue and site of the Opening Ceremony for the 1948 Games, Wembley will host the Football finals during the London 2012 Games. *Stadium Way, Wembley, Middx HA9 0WS (0844 980 8001, www.wembleystadium.com). Wembley Park tube or Wembley Stadium rail.*

66 Southbank Centre

Opened in 1951 as the centrepiece of the Festival of Britain, the Royal Festival Hall was wonderfully refurbished a few years back. Now the bars and restaurants – many of which look out over the Thames – hum with life all day. Under artistic director Jude Kelly, the programming has really come to life too, mixing cult bands and fun musicals with string quartets and classical concerts, and children's events with readings from august novelists. Next door to the RFH, the Queen Elizabeth Hall and Purcell Room host recitals and smaller events, while the Hayward Gallery displays changing exhibitions of contemporary art – one of which put a swimming pool on the gallery's roof for summer 2010.

South Bank, Belvedere Road, SE1 8XX (7960 4200, www.southbankcentre.co.uk). Embankment tube or Waterloo tube/rail.

67 Portobello Market

Famed for its antiques and collectibles, this is actually several markets rolled into one. The Saturday antiques market starts at the Notting Hill end; further up are food stalls and, under the Westway and along the walkway to Ladbroke Grove, emerging designers and vintage clothes dealers (Fridays and Saturdays, with Friday the less frantic of the two). Carry cash, as the cashpoint on the main drag is invariably mobbed.
Portobello Road, W10 (www.portobellomarket.org). Ladbroke Grove or Notting Hill Gate tube.

68 Hampton Court Palace

Everyone seems to fall in love with this spectacular red-brick palace. It was built in 1514 by Cardinal Wolsey, but Henry VIII liked it so much that he seized it in 1528. Even dour Oliver Cromwell took a shine to the place, moving in after the Civil War. Elizabeth I was probably less keen: she was imprisoned here by her elder sister Mary.

Just strolling through the courtyards and corridors is a pleasure, but there are plenty of highlights. The Great Hall, part of Henry VIII's State Apartments, is famed for its beautiful stained-glass windows and intricate religious tapestries, while the King's Apartments have a splendid mural of Alexander the Great, painted by Antonio Verrio. The Queen's Apartments and Georgian Rooms feature similarly elaborate paintings, chandeliers and tapestries. Listen out for the ghost of Catherine Howard – Henry's fifth wife, executed for adultery in 1542 – shrieking in the Haunted Gallery, or explore the Tudor Kitchens: their giant cauldrons and smoke-blackened fireplaces are regularly brought to life with cookery demonstrations, recreating centuries-old recipes.

Outside, the exquisitely landscaped gardens feature superb topiary, an ancient vine, peaceful Thames views, a reconstruction of a 16th-century heraldic garden and the famous Hampton Court maze.

East Molesey, Surrey KT8 9AU (0844 482 7777, www.hrp.org.uk). Hampton Court rail, or riverboat from Westminster or Richmond to Hampton Court Pier (Apr-Oct).

69 Madame Tussauds

Limber up for the London 2012 Games with a visit to the pantheon of sporting greats in the Sports Zone at Madame Tussauds: Lewis Hamilton and Muhammad Ali won't be taking part, but seeing them here might provide inspiration. In addition to getting snapped with the stars, you can score a penalty goal or test your driving reactions using fun interactives. Other zones introduce you to film, pop and TV celebs, while the 'Scream' attraction uses every special effect in the book, including floor drops, to make you quiver. Book online to avoid the enormous main queue and to save on the steep admission prices.

Marylebone Road, NW1 5LR (0870 400 3000, www.madame tussauds.com/london). Baker Street tube.

70 British Library

The British Library isn't just for scholars. Up the stairs to the left of the main entrance (be prepared to open your bags for the tiresome but necessary security check) is a room of bookish treasures. The free, changing display in the John Ritblat Gallery combines extraordinary historical artefacts – the Magna Carta, perhaps, with its cascade of wax seals, or a priceless Shakespeare First Folio – with such curios as handwritten lyrics from the Beatles or a Buddhist sutra dating back to the 1200s. There's sometimes an entry fee for the impressive temporary exhibitions downstairs.

96 Euston Road, NW1 2DB (7412 7332, www.bl.uk).
Euston or King's Cross tube/rail.

71 Splash out at London's department stores

While lesser shops come and go, the bastions of London's shopping scene remain its mighty department stores, which battle for shoppers' affections with all manner of retail thrills. **Liberty** (Regent Street, W1B 5AH, 7734 1234, www.liberty.co.uk; pictured) pairs sweetly old-fashioned premises with cutting-edge fashion: Erdem, Sessùn and APC are among the labels, exclusive designer collaborations abound, and accessories run from vertiginous Manolo Blahnik heels to classic Liberty-print diaries.

Selfridges (400 Oxford Street, W1A 1AB, 0800 123 4000, www. selfridges.com) is another fashionista favourite, famed for its extravagant window installations: Santa on a scooter, a Mad Hatter's tea party and a herd of galloping zebras have all featured in the past. Inside, delights include the extraordinary Shoe Galleries, which showcase over 4,000 shoes in a series of sumptuous boutiques.

Over in Knightsbridge, doormen in peaked caps open the doors into **Harrods** (87-135 Brompton Road, SW1X 7XL, 7730 1234, www.harrods. com), awash with marble, gilt sphinxes and ladies with poodles. But beyond the ostentation there is some seriously good shopping: the lingerie department stocks gorgeous pieces from the likes of Nina Ricci and Agent Provocateur, while the Denim Lounge is chock-full of hip brands. On the ground floor, the food hall is a cornucopia of delicacies, while Ladurée's tearoom is as exquisite as its famous macaroons. A stone's throw away, **Harvey Nichols** (109-125 Knightsbridge, SW1X 7RJ, 7235 5000, www. harveynichols.com) offers polished service and eight floors of beauty, fashion, homeware and food. Don't miss the concept store-inspired fourth floor, which mixes pieces by emerging British designers with vintage magazines, cult toys and a 'Sneaker Wall' that showcases designs by Christian Louboutin, Beatrix Ong and other big names.

More down-to-earth than its rivals, **John Lewis** (300 Oxford Street, W1A 1EX, 7629 7711, www.johnlewis.co.uk) remains dear to Londoners' hearts. Kitchenware, white goods and haberdashery are among its traditional strengths, although its fashion and beauty collections have become more directional of late; it's also the official department store for the London 2012 Games, with a dedicated fifth-floor shop.

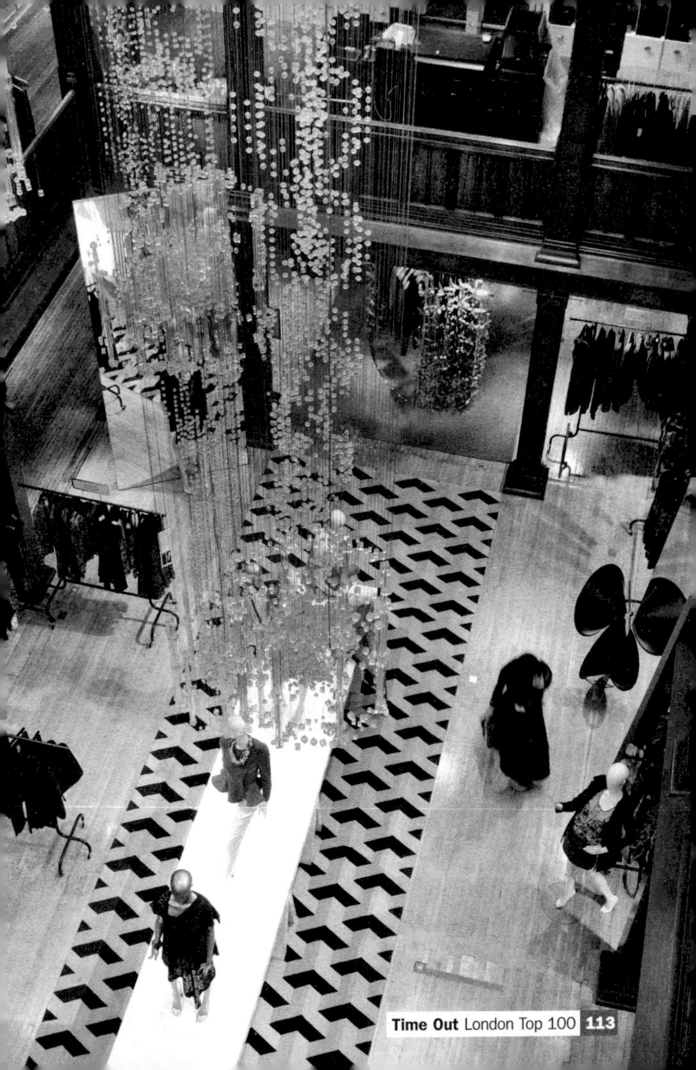

72 Lates

Imagine a museum free of children that can be explored with a glass of wine in hand. Over the last few years, special Lates events (www.lates.org) have enabled visitors to do just that, and have become a monthly fixture at 15 of London's finest museums and galleries. The format is similar whether you're at the National Gallery or the Museum of London (pictured), with a programme – often themed to tie in with the current blockbuster exhibition – combining DJs or live music, talks, perhaps a film screening, certainly a pay bar, and reduced ticket prices.

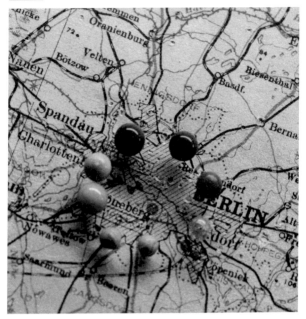

This cramped subterranean bunker was where Winston Churchill plotted Allied strategy in World War II, out of reach of the German bombers. Sealed off on 16 August 1945, its rooms exist in a state of suspended animation under the feet of Whitehall's shuffling bureaucrats. Every pin stuck into the vast charts was placed there in the final days of the conflict, as Churchill planned the end game to the war. Open to the public since 1984, the bunker powerfully brings to life the reality of a nation at war, with plenty of information on Churchill and his rousing speeches.
Clive Steps, King Charles Street, SW1A 2AQ (7930 6961, http://cwr.iwm.org.uk). St James's Park or Westminster tube.

74 Hunterian Museum

Now displayed in ultra-modern, backlit glass cabinets, 18th-century anatomist John Hunter's vast collection of medical specimans is mind-bogglingly macabre. Diseased body parts, a two-tailed lizard, the skull of a two-headed boy and a set of premature quintuplets, dating from 1786, are among the exhibits, along with Sir Winston Churchill's dentures. **Royal College of Surgeons, 35-43 Lincoln's Inn Fields, WC2A 3PE (7869 6560, www.rcseng.ac.uk/museums). Holborn tube.**

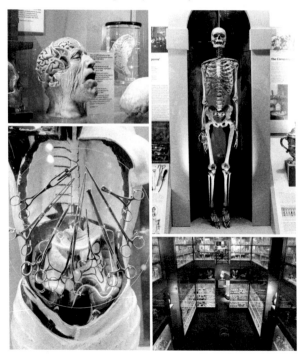

75 The Tates

Connected by the River Thames, Tate Modern and Tate Britain are two of the finest art galleries in the country. **Tate Britain** (Millbank, SW1P 4RG, 7887 8000, www.tate.org.uk) is the original – its stately Portland stone building has looked out over the Thames near Pimlico tube since 1897. Exhibits include a superb gallery of Turners, as well as works by Hogarth, Constable, Lucian Freud and Francis Bacon.

Tate Modern (Bankside, SE1 9TG, 7887 8888, www.tate.org.uk) is the more high-profile – and busier. It opened in a bold conversion of a riverside power station in 2000, and has been

immensely popular ever since – so much so that an ambitious new extension is being built. Covering every significant international movement of 20th-century art, the gallery's highlights include Monet's *Water-Lilies* and an untitled Rothko in Room 7, and Picasso's *The Three Dancers* and Matisse's *The Snail* in Room 5. Admission to both Tates is free, but their blockbuster temporary exhibitions usually charge an entry fee.

76 Covent Garden

This long-time tourist favourite has recently begun to draw in the locals too. The reopening of the London Transport Museum has been followed by the arrival of some impeccably cool shopping options (a huge Apple Store and singer Lily Allen's vintage boutique Lucy in Disguise both opened here in 2010), while the street entertainers that perform around the historic covered market building, especially under the portico of St Paul's church, hold the crowds enthralled. For more on the area's attractions and history, have a look at www.coventgardenlondonuk.com.

▶ *Trams, horse-drawn buses and resplendent double-deckers are among the collection at the London Transport Museum; see no.93.*

Guards Parade & anging of the Guard

rafalgar Square, an unsmiling young sentry under
ig atop a mighty horse. Welcome to Horse Guards
e of London's talent for military pageantry. Every
0am on Sundays), in the Parade Ground on the St
, the Changing of the Guard is a stately display of
synchro and immaculate uniforms: scarlet coats, polished
boots, sabres and cuirasses (breastplates). Strange to think that this will
be the site of the Beach Volleyball competition at the London 2012 Games.

Watching the parade is free, but to learn more about the Horse Guards,
pay the admission charge to enter the fine little Household Cavalry
Museum. Inside, as well as memorabilia and video diaries from the
soldiers, there are glass screens that allow you to look into the stables
and see the magnificent steeds being groomed.

On alternate days, the guard is also changed at nearby Buckingham
Palace. Here you'll see regiments of Foot Guards wearing tall bearskin
hats; it tends to be more crowded than Horse Guards, though, and fences
keep you at a distance from much of the action.

Horse Guards, Whitehall, SW1A 2AX (7930 3070,
www.householdcavalrymuseum.co.uk). Westminster
tube or Charing Cross tube/rail.

▶ *For more on visiting Buckingam Palace, see no.89.*

78 Regent's Park

St James's Park may be prettier, but the sheer size of **Regent's Park** (7298 2000, www.royalparks.org.uk) makes it wonderfully varied. On one side there's a busy waterfowl pond and a boating lake with an island where herons nest; on the other, a lovely rose garden. Several areas are dedicated to formal and informal sport, while the Camden side of the park is home to family favourite ZSL London Zoo (see no.4). From May to September, the **Open Air Theatre** (0844 826 4242, www.openair theatre.org) produces classic musicals and Shakespearean comedies.

79 | Sadler's Wells

Sadler's Wells is one of the best places in London to see dance performances – and the city's most important space dedicated to the art form. The work on show is rich and varied, from reworkings of classical ballet to abstract contemporary works, taking in hip hop, flamenco, tango and more.

Rosebery Avenue, EC1R 4TN (0844 412 4300, www.sadlerswells.com). Angel tube.

80 Westminster Abbey & the Houses of Parliament

A UNESCO-designated World Heritage Site, the collection of historic buildings around Parliament Square is undeniably impressive – regardless of how many times you've seen it in holidays snaps.

Westminster tube exits in the shadow of the Big Ben clocktower (Big Ben is the name of the largest bell within, not the tower itself). The intricately worked, tobacco-coloured **Houses of Parliament** (Parliament Square, SW1A 0AA, 7219 4272 Commons information, 7219 3107 Lords information, www.parliament.uk) then march away south along the Thames until they reach Victoria Tower Gardens, which has several interesting monuments (Rodin's *The Burghers of Calais*, a statue of suffragette Emmeline Pankhurst and the gaily coloured Buxton Memorial Fountain to the Emancipation of the Slaves). Parliament was extensively remodelled in the 1840s, but Westminster Hall retains its magnificent 14th-century hammer-beam roof; the only way to see it is to take one of the tours that run during Parliament's summer recess.

The south side of the Parliament Square is dominated by the flying buttresses of **Westminster Abbey** (20 Dean's Yard, SW1P 3PA, 7222 5152 information, 7654 4900 tours, www.westminster-abbey.org), within which almost every English monarch has been crowned since the 11th century. Elizabeth I and Mary, Queen of Scots, are buried here, and Poets' Corner commemorates writers as varied as Tennyson, Henry James and Dylan Thomas.

A heady whiff of drink, debauchery and rock 'n' roll excess still clings to Camden – long a stomping ground for guitar-toting musicians. Heading up towards Chalk Farm, the **Barfly** (49 Chalk Farm Road, NW1 8AN, 7888 8994, www.barfly club.com) is a well-established showcase for new bands, some of whom are destined for great things: Franz Ferdinand, Coldplay and the Strokes all played early gigs on its tiny stage. On the same road, the laid-back **Lock Tavern** (35 Chalk Farm Road, NW1 8AJ, 7482 7163, www.lock-tavern.co.uk) pairs good pub grub with an eclectic line-up of DJs and bands: Justice, Vampire Weekend and Disco Bloodbath have all performed here.

On the other side of the road, in the Grade II-listed Horse Hospital,

Proud (Stables Market, NW1 8AH, 7482 3867, www.proudcamu.
plays indie-electro and synth pop to assorted bright young things,
DJs and gigs almost every night of the week.

Towards Chalk Farm Tube, the **Roundhouse** (Chalk Farm Road, NW1
8EH, 7424 9991, www.roundhouse.org.uk) is a vibrant cultural hub,
housed in a converted Victorian engine shed. Rising stars, international
DJs and pop and rock legends all grace the stage, as part of a broader
remit that also takes in poetry, performing arts and circus extravaganzas.

Heading into Camden proper, there are myriad pubs and music venues.
Amy Winehouse is among the regulars at the **Hawley Arms** (2
Castlehaven Road, NW1 8QU, 7428 5979, www.thehawleyarms.co.uk);
for a more peaceful pint, try the cosy **Crown & Goose** (100 Arlington
Road, NW1 7HP, 7485 8008, www.crownandgoose.co.uk), which also
serves very decent food. On nearby Parkway, which is dotted with pubs
and restaurants, the **Jazz Café** (5-7 Parkway, NW1 7PG, 7485 6834,
www.jazzcafe.co.uk) offers a polished evening out. For more raucous club
nights and gigs, head for **Koko** (1A Camden High Street, NW1 7JE, 0870
432 5527, www.koko.uk.com) – an ornate former music hall with a
magnificent tiered interior and glittering chandeliers.

Taking in a chaotic cross-section of Camden life, the **Camden Crawl**
(www.thecamdencrawl.com) is a weekend-long, multi-venue music festival,
held in early May. It attracts a healthy mix of established headliners and
breakthrough acts – although with crowds piling in to see the bigger
names, you won't have much room for moshing.

▶ *In the daytime, Camden Market is the big draw. It's great for
people-watching, even if you don't make any puchases; see no.37.*

...lgar Square

...320s and named in honour of Nelson's famous victory, ... quare is the heart of modern London. Above it towers ...mn, topped with a statue of the valiant vice admiral – often ...spectful pigeon perched upon his head. Far below Nelson's ... .hree lower plinths are occupied by statues of George IV and Victo... military heroes. The fourth plinth is given over to temporary art installations. Featured artists have included Mark Quinn, Thomas

Schütte and Anthony Gormley, whose *One & Other* invited 2,400 members of the public to stand atop the plinth for an hour.

The square is both a place of protest and of celebration; on 8 May 1945, huge crowds gathered here to listen to Churchill's broadcast announcing victory in Europe. Throughout the year, a busy programme of events feature food stalls, music, dancers and parades: in October or November, the Diwali festival of light is always spectacular, while Christmas brings carol singers and a towering Norwegian spruce, swathed in twinkling lights. For full details of what's on, visit www.london.gov.uk/trafalgarsquare.

83 Natural History Museum

Generations of children have stood in the soaring central hall here, gazing up at the enormous diplodocus (nicknamed 'Dippy' by staff). A newer addition to the museum's prehistoric menagerie is its animatronic T-Rex, also on the ground floor, whose baleful eyes, swishing tail and throaty roars send younger visitors running for cover. Smaller beasts are covered here too, though – not least the leaf-cutting ants of the Creepy Crawlies gallery, toiling away in an enormous, glass-walled formicary.

Exhibits in the geology-focused Red zone include a ground-shaking earthquake simulator and chunks of moon rock, precious metals and glow-in-the-dark minerals, while the Orange zone takes in a wildlife garden and the eight-storey Darwin Centre, which opened in 2009. The centre's vast, cocoon-shaped structure is a marvel in itself; venture inside to watch scientists at work in state-of-the-art laboratories and see some weird and wonderful plant and insect specimans.

Cromwell Road, SW7 5BD (7942 5000, www.nhm.ac.uk).
South Kensington tube.

84 Ripley's Believe It or Not!

Although admission prices are steep, children will delight in this five-floor 'odditorium', which is devoted to all things strange, spooky and sometimes downright freaky. A shrunken head from Ecuador and a two-headed calf vie for visitors' attentions with medieval torture devices and a smoking reconstruction of an electric chair; less grisly oddities include a statue of the Beatles made from chewing gum, Marilyn Monroe's make-up bag and Leonardo's *Last Supper*, painted on a grain of rice. Tackle the Vortex – a giddying contraption involving a bridge and a spinning kaleidoscope – at your peril, and preferably before having lunch.
**1 Piccadilly Circus, W1J 0DA (3238 0022, www.ripleyslondon.com).
Piccadilly Circus tube.**

85 | Eat at a gastropub

Newer arrivals may have fancier dining rooms and smoother service, but the bold Mediterranean flavours and hefty portions at London's first gastropub, the **Eagle** (159 Farringdon Road, EC1R 3AL, 7837 1353; pictured above), mean it remains a firm favourite. With its mismatched wooden chairs, tumblers of red wine and pared-down menu, Southwark's **Anchor & Hope** (36 The Cut, SE1 8LP, 7928 9898) has a similarly casual vibe – and is only a short walk from Tate Modern (see no.75). You can't book, so there's often a wait in the bar before you can squeeze on to one of the communal tables and order up a feast: a rich, wintry cassoulet, perhaps, or arbroath smokies with cream and chives. Not far from Covent Garden, the Anchor's sister establishment, **Great Queen Street** (32 Great Queen Street, WC2B 5AA, 7242 0622; pictured right), does take bookings. Head chef Tom Norrington-Davies (formerly of the Eagle) produces some terrific specialities to share, including chicken pie for two or an immense, slow-cooked lamb shoulder that will feed four or more.

Over the last ten years, brothers Tom and Ed Martin have built up a flotilla of excellent gastropubs across London. One of their first was the **Gun** (27 Coldharbour, E14 9NS, 7515 5222, www.thegun docklands.com), on the Isle of Dogs. Not far from Canary Wharf, it stands across the river from the O2 Arena/North Greenwich Arena (see no.42), with great views from its terrace. The food is British and hearty: think potted Morecambe Bay shrimps, followed by pan-fried bream or roast partridge with stuffed cabbage.

A welcome and relatively recent addition to the city's panoply of gastropubs is Fulham's **Harwood Arms** (Walham Grove, SW6 1QP, 7386 1847, www.harwoodarms. com), whose chef scored a Michelin star in 2010. Getting a table isn't easy, but dishes like grilled fallow deer chops or the signature snails with stout-braised oxtail and bone marrow are well worth the wait.

86 Royal Academy of Arts

The grand, Palladian Burlington House makes a suitably dignified setting for the Royal Academy's headquarters. Free-entry shows run alongside ticketed blockbuster exhibitions, while the biggest event of the year remains the Summer Exhibition – a fixture since 1769. Works by illustrious Royal Academians (including the likes of David Hockney and Sarah Lucas) are shown alongside submissions by the general public; most are for sale, with prices starting from around £75 and climbing into six figures for the star pieces.

Burlington House, Piccadilly, W1J 0BD (7300 8000, www.royal academy.org.uk). Green Park or Piccadilly Circus tube.

87 | Highgate Cemetery

Opened in 1839, not long after Queen Victoria came to the throne, Highgate Cemetery is superbly atmospheric, with its crumbling Gothic monuments, blank-eyed angels and trailing ivy. The East Cemetery is open to the public daily (except when there is a burial) and contains the monument to Karl Marx, as well as the remains of novelists George Eliot and Douglas Adams; the West Cemetery is prettier, but can only be visited on a tour (children under eight are not allowed). Other famous occupants include physicist Michael Faraday, murdered Russian dissident Alexander Litvinenko, punk impresario Malcolm McLaren and a gaggle of Pre-Raphaelites – among them poet Christina Rossetti and Elizabeth Siddal, model for John Everett Millais's *Ophelia*.
Swain's Lane, Highgate, N6 6PJ (8340 1834, www.highgate-cemetery.org). Archway tube.

88 Lord's Cricket Ground

A sleepy summer's day at the spiritual home of cricket is one of London's sporting treats. The stadium is a surprisingly harmonious combination of a gracious red-brick Victorian pavilion and the futuristic white pod that houses the Media Centre, a marriage of old and new that will make the ground a fitting location for the Olympic Archery competition during the London 2012 Games. Tickets for international fixtures – whether the five-day Test matches beloved of connoisseurs, a single-day 50-over-a-

side match or the crash-bang-wallop excitement of a three-hour Twenty20 contest – are hard to come by unless you book well in advance. Better instead to attend domestic fixtures (this is the home ground of the Middlesex County Cricket Club) or book a place on one of the guided tours around the buildings and the MCC Museum. Memorabilia on display runs from the tiny Ashes urn and portraits of WG Grace to a stuffed sparrow, attached to the cricket ball that killed it in 1936.
St John's Wood Road, NW8 8QN (7616 8500, www.lords.org).
St John's Wood tube.

89 Buckingham Palace & the Royal Mews

To find out whether Her Majesty is in residence, check which flag is fluttering above the palace: if it's the Royal Standard rather than the Union Jack, she's at home. In August and September, she won't be. That's when the Queen visits Scotland – and the palace's 19 sumptuously appointed State Rooms are opened to the public.

For the rest of the year, admire family heirlooms in the Queen's Gallery, which contains paintings by Rubens and Rembrandt and some exquisite Sèvres porcelain

(George IV was a keen collector), or head to the Royal Mews to see the royal fleet of Bentleys and Rolls-Royces, along with the splendid carriages and the horses that pull them (the names of the Windsor greys are chosen by the Queen). *The Mall, SW1A 1AA (7766 7300, www.royalcollection. org.uk). Green Park tube or Victoria tube/rail.*
▶ *For a burst of regal pomp and ceremony, join the crowds that gather to watch the Changing of the Guard; see no.77.*

90 | Saatchi Gallery

A champion of the headline-grabbing Young British Artists of the 1990s (notably Damien Hirst and Tracey Emin), Charles Saatchi remains a prodigious collector of contemporary art.

Set in a huge converted military barracks just off the King's Road in Chelsea, the Saatchi Gallery showcases global art rather than focusing on the Brits. Changing exhibitions of contemporary art occupy its minimalist, white-painted galleries, featuring paintings and sculptures both by big names and lesser known talents. Look out, too, for longstanding favourites such as *20:50*, Richard Wilson's deceptively simple and visually spectacular sump-oil installation.

Duke of York's HQ, off King's Road, SW3 4SQ (7823 2363, www.saatchi-gallery.co.uk). Sloane Square tube.

91 Spend the day in Greenwich

Half the fun of a day out in Greenwich is getting here. Although you can catch the DLR, it's more exciting to take a Thames Clipper (see no.15) and disembark at Greenwich Pier, by the **Cutty Sark** (www.cuttysark. org.uk). This 19th-century tea clipper, once the fastest ship in the world, is under wraps for a massive renovation project, but should re-emerge in all her glory in time for the London 2012 Games.

After a meander through Greenwich Market's stalls and shops, head for the free-entry Discover Greenwich exhibition, set in the corner of the **Old Royal Naval College** (2 Cutty Sark Gardens, SE10 9LW, 8269 4799, www.oldroyalnavalcollege.org.uk) nearest the *Cutty Sark*. Artefacts and exhibits explore the area's rich history and imposing architecture (not for nothing is Greenwich a UNESCO-designated World Heritage Site), while children can build their own grand designs in soft bricks or try to lift a knight's jousting lance. The Naval College's other highlight is the splendid ceiling of the Painted Hall, which took Sir James Thornhill almost two decades to complete.

The vast white colonnades of the Naval College – which seem to shimmer when the sun is bright – were designed by Sir Christopher Wren to frame Inigo Jones' much more modest **Queen's House**, across the Romney Road. Completed in 1638, the house has an intriguing collection of seafaring art and a splendid interior court, tiled in black and white. It's run by the neighbouring **National Maritime Museum** (Romney Road, SE10 9NF, 8312 6565, www.nmm.ac.uk), whose immense collection of maritime maps, instruments and regalia includes the blood-stained jacket in which Nelson met his end. The interactive exhibits are in the Bridge and All Hands galleries, where you can load cargo, steer a ferry and try your hand as a ship's gunner.

Behind the museum stretches Greenwich Park – an ancient royal hunting ground that will host the Equestrian events during the London 2012 Games. It's a steep ten-minute hike across the park and up to the **Royal Observatory Greenwich** (8312 6565, www.rog.nmm.ac.uk), although there is also a shuttle bus. At the top you can straddle the Prime Meridian Line, marked on the courtyard's flagstones, then check out the 14th-century timekeeping equipment and 28-inch refracting telescope in Flamsteed House, built in 1675 for the first Astronomer Royal, Sir John Flamsteed. In addition to all these free attractions, you can pay to take in a spectacular star-show in the Peter Harrison Planetarium before re-emerging, blinking, into the daylight.

92 See a West End show

For a night of theatrical glitz and glamour the West End is still the place to go, with numerous big-budget shows running year-round. Productions change, of course, but you'll always find extravagant musical versions of blockbuster films, such as the touching *Billy Elliot the Musical* and the exuberant *Legally Blonde the Musical*. Then there are the 'jukebox' musicals, with narratives constructed around hit songs (the thoroughly enjoyable *Jersey Boys*, for example, which traces the career of Frankie Valli and the Four Seasons) and the 'proper' musicals, which include the lavish, long-running *Les Misérables* and *Phantom of the Opera*.

If ticket prices seem off-puttingly high, pay a visit to **Tkts** (Clocktower Building, WC2H 7NA, www.officiallondontheatre.co.uk/tkts), which occupies a stand-alone booth on the south side of Leicester Square. Operated by the Society of London Theatre, it sells tickets for many of the big shows at much-reduced rates, either on the day or up to a week in advance.

The West End's lavish productions are, of course, just one side of London's thriving theatre scene. For new plays and rising talents, head

for Chelsea's famously radical **Royal Court Theatre** (Sloane Square, SW1W 8AS, 7565 5000, www.royalcourttheatre.com); in recent years, several productions have transferred from its modest stage to the West End and beyond.

In Covent Garden, the **Donmar Warehouse** (41 Earlham Street, WC2H 9LX, 0844 871 7624, www.donmarwarehouse.com) is another place to catch shows before they hit the big time – and to see Hollywood stars honing their craft. Nicole Kidman, Ewan McGregor and Gwyneth Paltrow have all appeared on its tiny stage. Meanwhile, Kevin Spacey's role as artistic director at the **Old Vic** (The Cut, SE1 8NB, 0844 871 7628, www.oldvictheatre.com) ensures a sprinkling of big-name stars at this grand Victorian theatre.

93 London Transport Museum

A gleaming collection of vehicles brings the city's transport history to life, running from a jaunty little horse-drawn tram to increasingly sleek variations on the classic red bus. The collection of posters is superb, too, extolling Londoners to see the sights, do their Christmas shopping, join the war effort and say please and thank-you to London Underground staff; look out for a surreal design by Man Ray, dating from the 1930s.
Covent Garden Piazza, WC2E 7BB (7379 6344, www.ltmuseum. co.uk). Covent Garden tube.

94 Sip a cocktail

Drinking dens don't come much more sophisticated than the **Connaught Bar** (16 Carlos Place, W1K 2AL, 7499 7070, www.theconnaught.com), part of the equally swish Connaught Hotel. Sumptuous, 1920s-influenced decor provides the perfect backdrop for some stellar cocktails; the Connaught Martini is worth ordering for the table-side theatricals alone.

The art deco **American Bar at the Savoy** (100 Strand, WC2R 0EW, 7836 4343, www.fairmont.com/savoy) is another classic – and in sparkling form after the hotel's three-year refurbishment. In some ways, though, little has changed since its '20s heyday: jazz standards come courtesy of a tuxedo-clad pianist, the sleek curve of the bar is lined with gleaming bottles, and the cocktails pack a heady punch.

For more outré flavours, try **69 Colebrooke Row** (69 Colebrooke Row, N1 8AA, 07540 528593, www.69colebrookerow.com; pictured above), tucked away on an Islington backstreet. The premises are tiny, so it's advisable to call ahead to reserve a table if you want to sample cocktail maestro Tony Conigliaro's creations: a liquorice whisky sour, perhaps, or a fragrant, vodka-spiked Lipstick Rose.

Hidden away in a Marylebone basement, **Purl** (50 Blandford Street, W1U 7HX, 7935 0835, www.purl-london.com) is another delightfully quirky enterprise. Low lighting, leather chesterfields and swing jazz create a laid-back, inviting vibe, while ingenious concoctions on the cocktail menu include the Backwards Bellini, made with a lavender bitters-infused sugar cube, prosecco and pomegranate foam. Most come in at under £10, making this one of London's more affordable cocktail haunts.

▶ *For bespoke recommendations in stylish surrounds, book an early-evening table at Soho's Milk & Honey; see no.56.*

95 Sea Life London Aquarium

All aquatic life is here, from jauntily striped clown fish to endangered Cuban crocodiles. Starfish, crabs and anemones can be handled in special open rock pools, while the Shark Walk – they swim beneath your feet – provides a delicious frisson of danger. Book online (and for slots after 3pm) for cheaper tickets.
County Hall, Riverside Building, Westminster Bridge Road, SE1 7PB (0871 663 1678, www.sealife.co.uk). Westminster tube or Waterloo tube/rail.

96 Wellcome Collection

This wonderfully offbeat museum is based around the medical curios collected by globe-trotting 19th-century pharmacist Sir Henry Wellcome. Upstairs, the 'Medicine Man' room displays his fascinating and often macabre finds, which include ivory carvings of pregnant women, used guillotine blades, Napoleon's toothbrush and a Chinese torture chair. Next door, a second room examines modern medical matters with the help of attention-grabbing contemporary art.

Downstairs is a bookshop, a fine Peyton & Byrne café and a space for the always excellent temporary exhibitions. Themes like 'Identity', 'Skin' and 'High Society' (recreational drugs) are entertainingly explored, with associated special events that might run from walks and lectures to gigs, operettas and experiments.

183 Euston Road, NW1 2BE (7611 2222, www.wellcome collection.org). Euston Square tube or Euston tube/rail.

97 Columbia Road Market

Of a Sunday morning (8am-2pm), there's no lovelier place to be than this fragrant East End flower market. The street becomes a sea of blooms, packed with vibrant hothouse beauties, sweet-smelling stocks and bargain-priced bedding plants ('three for a fiver' is the stallholders' rallying cry). Galleries and boutiques also thrive here: look out for the nostalgic **Lapin & Me** (14 Ezra Street, E2 7RH, 7739 4384, www.lapinandme. co.uk), selling gifts and homeware, and the charming **Ryantown** (126 Columbia Road, E2 7RG, 7613 1510), where artist Rob Ryan sells his intricate paper-cut artworks and screenprints.

Call in at **Jones' Dairy** (23 Ezra Street, E2 7RH, 7739 5372, www. jonesdairy.co.uk) for coffee, cake and a take-home chunk of cheese, then watch as locals wobble homeward, olive trees perched precariously on their bike racks.

Columbia Road, E2 (www.columbiaroad.info). Hoxton rail or Liverpool Street tube/rail then bus 26, 48.

98 Royal Opera House

The Royal Opera and the Royal Ballet are both based at this soaring 19th-century opera house, making for a packed cultural programme. Meanwhile, daily backstage tours offer a peek behind the scenes – if you're lucky, you might catch members of the Royal Ballet practising their pirouettes. Otherwise, look out over the bustle of Covent Garden from the covered loggia of the Amphitheatre restaurant-bar, open from spring each year.

Covent Garden, WC2E 9DD (7304 4000, www.roh.org.uk). Covent Garden tube.

99 Notting Hill Carnival

For three days over the August bank holiday weekend, the streets of Notting Hill are taken over by Europe's largest street party (7727 0072, www.thenottinghillcarnival.com), attended by over a million revellers. Steel bands, pounding sound systems, Caribbean food stalls and plenty of rum punch are all thrown into the mix, while stilt-walkers, fabulous costumes, shimmying dancers and a generous quantity of sequins make the parades (the children's parade is held on Sunday, the adults' on Monday) a sight to remember.

For one weekend each September, Open House London (3006 7008, http://open-city.org.uk) allows visitors a glimpse inside hundreds of buildings that are normally out of bounds to the public. It's a hugely – and deservedly – popular event: if the glass and steel Lloyd's of London building is taking part, it usually has a queue snaking all along Leadenhall Street by mid morning, while demand was so high for the 2010 opening of the BT Tower that architecture buffs had to enter a ticket ballot.

Buildings might run from the former Fleet Street headquarters of the *Daily Express* (a sleek, art deco masterpiece) to the members-only London Library in St James's Square, along with Hindu temples, eco-friendly private abodes, state-of-the-art skyscrapers and dusty churches. No matter how well you know the city, there's always a corner still to explore – which is why we love this event.

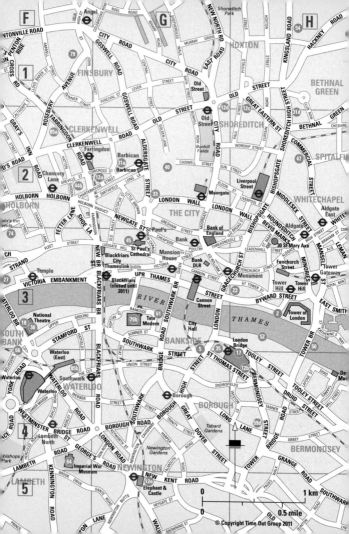

Venues shaded in grey either lie off the map or can't be plotted (for example, the Thames Clipper boat service). Bullet numbers correspond to the order in which venues appear in the book.

A-Z Index